"ALLEN REMAINS
A MASTER OF PARODY,
DAZZLING NONSEQUITURS AND
EVEN MANAGES A HILARIOUS
PSEUDO SCIENCE FICTION."
Boston Sunday Globe

CONTENTS

Also by Woody Allen
Published by Ballantine Books

WITHOUT FEATHERS

SIDE EFFECTS

Woody Allen

BALLANTINE BOOKS • NEW YORK

"Retribution" and "The Shallowest Man" originally appeared
in *The Kenyon Review*.
"The Lunatic's Tale," "Nefarious Times We Live In," "The
Query" and "Remembering Needleman" originally appeared in
The New Republic.
"My Speech to the Graduates" originally appeared in *The
New York Times*.
The following stories originally appeared in *The New Yorker*:
"By Destiny Denied," "The Condemned," "The Diet," "Fabri-
zio's: Criticism and Response," "A Giant Step for Mankind,"
"The Kugelmass Episode," "Reminiscences: Places and Peo-
ple," "The UFO Menace," and "Confessions of a Burglar."

Library of Congress Catalog Card Number: 79-5549

ISBN 0-345-33432-9

This edition published by arrangement with Random House,
Inc.

Manufactured in the United States of America

First Ballantine Books Edition: September 1981
Seventh Printing: October 1985

Contents

Remembering
Needleman

IT HAS BEEN four weeks and it is still hard for me to believe Sandor Needleman is dead. I was present at the cremation and at his son's request, brought the marshmallows, but few of us could think of anything but our pain.

Needleman was constantly obsessing over his funeral plans and once told me, "I much prefer cremation to burial in the earth, and both to a weekend with Mrs. Needleman." In the end, he chose to have himself cremated and donated his ashes to the University of Heidelberg, which scattered them to the four winds and got a deposit on the urn.

I can still see him with his crumpled suit and grey sweater. Preoccupied with weighty matters, he frequently would forget to remove the coat hanger from his jacket while he wore it. I reminded him of it one time at a Princeton Commencement and he smiled calmly and said,

"Good, let those who have taken issue with my theories think at least that I have broad shoulders." Two days later he was committed to Bellevue for doing a sudden back somersault in the midst of a conversation with Stravinsky.

Needleman was not an easily understood man. His reticence was mistaken for coldness, but he was capable of great compassion, and after witnessing a particularly horrible mine disaster once, he could not finish a second helping of waffles. His silence, too, put people off, but he felt speech was a flawed method of communication and he preferred to hold even his most intimate conversations with signal flags.

When he was dismissed from the faculty of Columbia University for his controversy with the then head of the school, Dwight Eisenhower, he waited for the renowned ex-general with a carpet beater and pelted him until Eisenhower ran for cover into a toy store. (The two men had a bitter public disagreement over whether the class bell signaled the end of a period or the beginning of another.)

Needleman had always hoped to die a quiet death. "Amidst my books and papers like my brother Johann." (Needleman's brother had suffocated under a rolltop desk while searching for his rhyming dictionary.)

Who would have thought that while Needleman would be watching the demolition of a building on his lunch hour, he would be tapped in the head by a wrecking ball? The blow caused massive shock and Needleman expired with a broad smile. His last, enigmatic words were, "No thanks, I already own a penguin."

As always, at the time of Needleman's death he was at work on several things. He was creating an Ethics, based on his theory that "good and just behavior is not only more moral but could be done by phone." Also, he was halfway through a new study of semantics, proving (as he so violently insisted) that sentence structure is innate but that whining is acquired. Finally, yet another book on the Holocaust. This one with cutouts. Needleman had always been obsessed by the problem of evil and argued quite eloquently that true evil was only possible if its perpetrator was named Blackie or Pete. His own flirtation with National Socialism caused a scandal in academic circles, though despite everything from gymnastics to dance lessons, he could not master the goose step.

Nazism was for him merely a reaction against academic philosophy, a position he always attempted to impress on friends and then would grab at their faces with feigned excitement and say, "Aha! Got your nose." It is easy to criticize his position on Hitler at first, but one must take into account his own philosophical writings. He had rejected contemporary ontology and insisted that man existed prior to infinity though not with too many options. He differentiated between existence and Existence, and knew one was preferable, but could never remember which. Human freedom for Needleman consisted of being aware of the absurdity of life. "God is silent," he was fond of saying, "now if we can only get Man to shut up."

Authentic Being, reasoned Needleman, could only be achieved on weekends and even then it required the borrowing of a car. Man, according to Needleman, was not a "thing" apart from nature, but was involved "in nature," and could not observe his own existence without first pretending to be indifferent and then running around to the opposite end of the room quickly in the hopes of glimpsing himself.

His term for the life process was *Angst Zeit,* loosely meaning Anxiety-Time and suggested man was a creature doomed to exist in "time" even though that was not where the action was. After much reflection, Needleman's intellectual integrity convinced him that he didn't exist, his friends didn't exist, and the only thing that was real was his IOU to the bank for six million marks. Hence, he was charmed by the National Socialist's philosophy of power, or as Needleman put it, "I have the kind of eyes that are set off by a brown shirt." After it became apparent that National Socialism was just the type of menace that Needleman stood against, he fled Berlin. Disguised as a bush and moving sideways only, three quick paces at a time, he crossed the border without being noticed.

Everywhere in Europe Needleman went, students and intellectuals were eager to help him, awed by his reputation. On the run, he found time to publish *Time, Essence, and Reality: A Systematic Reevaluation of Nothingness* and his delightful lighter treatise, *The Best Places to Eat While in Hiding*. Chaim Weizmann and Martin Buber took up a collection and obtained signed petitions to permit Needleman to emigrate to the United States, but at the time the hotel of his choice was full. With German soldiers minutes from his hideout in Prague, Needleman decided to come to America after all, but a scene occurred at the airport when he was overweight with his luggage. Albert Einstein, who was on that same flight, explained to him that if he would just remove the shoe trees from his shoes he could take everything. The two frequently corresponded after that. Einstein once wrote him, "Your work and my work are very similar although I'm still not exactly sure what your work is."

Once in America, Needleman was rarely out of public controversy. He published his famous, *Non-Existence: What To Do If It Suddenly Strikes You*. Also the classic work on linguistic philosophy, *Semantic Modes of Non-Essential Functioning*, which was made into the hit movie, *They Flew By Night*.

Typically, he was asked to resign from Harvard because of his affiliation with the Communist party. He felt only in a system with no economic inequality could there be real freedom and cited as the model society an ant farm. He could observe ants for hours and used to muse wistfully, "They're truly harmonious. If only their women were prettier they'd have it made." Interestingly, when Needleman was called by the House Un-American Activities Committee, he named names and justified it to his friends by citing his philosophy: "Political actions have no moral consequences but exist outside of the realm of true Being." For once the academic community stood chastened and it was not until weeks later that the faculty at Princeton decided to tar and feather Needleman. Needleman, incidentally, used this same reasoning to justify his concept of free love, but neither of two young coeds would buy it and the sixteen-year-old blew the whistle on him.

Needleman was passionate about the halting of nuclear testing and flew to Los Alamos, where he and several students refused to remove themselves from the site of a scheduled atomic detonation. As minutes ticked off and it became apparent the test would proceed as planned, Needleman was heard to mutter, "Uh-oh," and made a run for it. What the newspapers did not print was that he had not eaten all day.

It is easy to remember the public Needleman. Brilliant, committed, the author of *Styles of Modes*. But it is the private Needleman I will always fondly recall, the Sandor Needleman who was never without some favorite hat. Indeed, he was cremated with a hat on. A first, I believe. Or the Needleman who loved Walt Disney movies so passionately and who, despite lucid explanations of animation by Max Planck, could not be dissuaded from putting in a person-to-person call to Minnie Mouse.

When Needleman was staying at my house as a guest, I knew he liked a particular brand of tuna fish. I stocked the guest kitchen with it. He was too shy to admit his fondness for it to me, but once, thinking he was alone, opened every can and mused, "You are all my children."

At the opera in Milan with my daughter and me, Needleman leaned out of his box and fell into the orchestra pit. Too proud to admit it was a mistake, he attended the opera every night for a month and repeated it each time. Soon he developed a mild brain concussion. I pointed out that he could stop falling as his point had been made. He said, "No. A few more times. It's really not so bad."

I remember Needleman's seventieth birthday. His wife bought him pajamas. Needleman was obviously disappointed as he had hinted for a new Mercedes. Still, it is the mark of the man that he retired to the study and had his tantrum privately. He reentered the party smiling and wore the pajamas to the opening night of two short plays by Arabel.

The Condemned

BRISSEAU WAS ASLEEP in the moonlight. Lying on his back in bed, with his fat stomach jutting into the air and his mouth forming an inane smile, he appeared to be some kind of inanimate object, like a large football or two tickets to the opera. A moment later, when he rolled over and the moonlight seemed to strike him from a different angle, he looked exactly like a twenty-seven-piece starter set of silverware, complete with salad bowl and soup tureen.

He's dreaming, Cloquet thought, as he stood over him, revolver in hand. *He's* dreaming, and I exist in reality. Cloquet hated reality but realized it was still the only place to get a good steak. He had never taken a human life before. True, he had once shot a mad dog, but only after it had been certified as mad by a team of psychiatrists. (The dog was diagnosed as manic-depressive after it had tried to bite off Cloquet's nose and then could not stop laughing.)

In his dream, Brisseau was on a sunlit beach and running joyously toward his mother's outstretched arms, but just as he began to embrace the weeping grey-haired woman, she turned into two scoops of vanilla ice cream. Brisseau moaned and Cloquet lowered the revolver. He had entered through the window and stood poised over Brisseau for more than two hours, unable to pull the trigger. Once, he had even cocked the hammer and placed the muzzle of the gun right in Brisseau's left ear. Then there was a sound at the door, and Cloquet leaped behind the bureau, leaving the pistol sticking out of Brisseau's ear.

Madame Brisseau, who was wearing a flowered bathrobe, entered the room, turned on a small lamp, and noticed the weapon protruding straight up out of the side of her husband's head. Almost maternally, she sighed and removed it, placing it beside the pillow. She tucked in a loose corner of the quilt, snapped off the lamp, and left.

Cloquet, who had fainted, awoke an hour later. For one panicky moment, he imagined he was a child again, back on the Riviera, but after fifteen minutes went by and he saw no tourists it came to him that he was still behind Brisseau's chest of drawers. He returned to the bed, seized the pistol, and again pointed it at Brisseau's head, but he was still unable to squeeze off the shot that would end the life of the infamous Fascist informer.

Gaston Brisseau came from a wealthy, right-wing family, and decided early in life to become a professional informer. As a young man, he took speech lessons so that he could inform more clearly. Once, he had confessed to Cloquet, "God, I enjoy tattling on people."

"But why?" Cloquet said.

"I don't know. Getting them in Dutch, squealing."

Brisseau ratted on his friends for the pure sake of it, Cloquet thought. Unredeemable evil! Cloquet had once known an Algerian who loved smacking people on the back of the head and then smiling and denying it. It seemed the world was divided into good and bad people. The good ones slept better, Cloquet thought, while the bad ones seemed to enjoy the waking hours much more.

Cloquet and Brisseau had met years before, under dramatic circumstances. Brisseau had gotten drunk at the Deux Magots one night and staggered toward the river. Thinking he was already home in his apartment, he removed his clothes, but instead of getting into bed he got into the Seine. When he tried to pull the blankets over himself and got a handful of water, he began screaming. Cloquet, who at that moment happened to be chasing his toupee across the Pont-Neuf, heard a cry from the icy water. The night was windy and dark, and Cloquet had a split second to decide if he would risk his life to save a stranger. Unwilling to make such a momentous decision on an empty stomach, he went to a res-

15

taurant and dined. Then, stricken with remorse, he purchased some fishing tackle and returned to fish Brisseau out of the river. At first he tried a dry fly, but Brisseau was too clever to bite, and in the end Cloquet was forced to coax Brisseau to shore with an offer of free dance lessons and then land him with a net. While Brisseau was being measured and weighed, the two became friends.

Now Cloquet stepped closer to Brisseau's sleeping hulk and again cocked the pistol. A feeling of nausea swept over him as he contemplated the implications of his action. This was an existential nausea, caused by his intense awareness of the contingency of life, and could not be relieved with an ordinary Alka-Seltzer. What was required was an Existential Alka-Seltzer—a product sold in many Left Bank drugstores. It was an enormous pill, the size of an automobile hubcap, that, dissolved in water, took away the queasy feeling induced by too much awareness of life. Cloquet had also found it helpful after eating Mexican food.

If I choose to kill Brisseau, Cloquet thought now, I am defining myself as a murderer. I will become Cloquet who kills, rather than simply what I am: Cloquet who teaches Psychology of Fowl at the Sorbonne. By choosing my action, I choose it for all mankind. But what if everyone in the world behaved like me and came here and shot Brisseau through the ear? What a mess! Not to mention the commotion from the doorbell ringing all night. And of course we'd need valet parking. Ah, God, how the mind boggles when it turns to moral or ethical considerations! Better not to think too much. Rely more on the body— the body is more dependable. It shows up for meetings, it looks good in a sports jacket, and where it really comes in handy is when you want to get a rubdown.

Cloquet felt a sudden need to reaffirm his own existence, and looked into the mirror over Brisseau's bureau. (He could never pass a mirror without sneaking a peek, and once at a health club he had stared at his reflection in a swimming pool for so long that the management was forced to drain it.) It was no use. He couldn't shoot a man. He dropped the pistol and fled.

Out on the street, he decided to go to La Coupole for a brandy. He liked La Coupole because it was always bright and crowded, and he could usually get a table—quite a difference from his own apartment, where it was dark and gloomy and where his mother, who lived there, too, always refused to seat him. But tonight La Coupole was filled. Who are all these faces, Cloquet wondered. They seem to blur into an abstraction: "The People." But there are no people, he thought—only individuals. Cloquet felt this was a brilliant perception, one that he could use impressively at some chic dinner party. Because of observations such as this, he had not been invited to a social gathering of any sort since 1931.

He decided to go to Juliet's house.

"Did you kill him?" she asked as he entered her flat.

"Yes," Cloquet said.

"Are you sure he is dead?"

"He seemed dead. I did my imitation of Maurice Chevalier, and it usually gets a big hand. This time, nothing."

"Good. Then he'll never betray the Party again."

Juliet was a Marxist, Cloquet reminded himself. And the most interesting type of Marxist—the kind with long, tanned legs. She was one of the few women he knew who could hold two disparate concepts in her mind at once, such as Hegel's dialectic and why if you stick your tongue in a man's ear while he is making a speech he will start to sound like Jerry Lewis. She stood before him now in a tight skirt and blouse, and he wanted to possess her—to own her the way he owned any other object, such as his radio or the rubber pig mask he had worn to harass the Nazis during the Occupation.

Suddenly he and Juliet were making love—or was it merely sex? He knew there was a difference between sex and love, but felt that either act was wonderful unless one of the partners happened to be wearing a lobster bib. Women, he reflected, were a soft, enveloping presence. Existence was a soft, enveloping presence, too. Sometimes it enveloped you totally. Then you could never get out again except for something really important, like your mother's birthday or jury duty. Cloquet often thought there was a great difference between Being and Being-in-the-World, and figured that no matter which group he belonged to the other was definitely having more fun.

He slept well after the lovemaking, as usual, but the next morning, to his great surprise, he was arrested for the murder of Gaston Brisseau.

At police headquarters, Cloquet protested his innocence, but he was informed that his fingerprints had been found all over Brisseau's room and on the recovered pistol. When he broke into Brisseau's house, Cloquet had also made the mistake of signing the guestbook. It was hopeless. The case was open-and-shut.

The trial, which took place over the following weeks, was like a circus, although there was some difficulty getting the elephants into the courtroom. At last, the jury found Cloquet guilty, and he was sentenced to the guillotine. An appeal for clemency was turned down on a technicality when it was learned Cloquet's lawyer had filed it while wearing a cardboard mustache.

Six weeks later, on the eve of his execution, Cloquet sat alone in his cell, still unable to believe the events of the past months—particularly the part about the elephants in the courtroom. By this time the next day, he would be dead. Cloquet had always thought of death as something that happened to other people. "I notice it happens to fat people a lot," he told his lawyer. To Cloquet himself, death seemed to be only another abstraction. Men die, he thought, but does Cloquet die? This question puzzled him, but a few simple line drawings on a pad done by one of the guards set the whole thing clear. There was no evading it. Soon he would no longer exist.

I will be gone, he thought wistfully, but Madame Plotnick, whose face looks like something on the menu in a seafood restaurant, will still be around. Cloquet began to panic. He wanted to run and hide, or, even better, to become something solid and durable—a heavy chair, for instance. A chair has no problems, he thought. It's there; nobody bothers it. It doesn't have to pay rent or get involved politically. A chair can never stub its toe or misplace its earmuffs. It doesn't have to smile or get a haircut, and you never have to worry that if you take it to a party it will suddenly start coughing or make a scene. People just sit in a chair, and then when those people die other people sit in it. Cloquet's logic comforted him, and when the jailers came at dawn to shave his neck, he pretended to be a chair. When they asked him what he wanted for his last meal, he said, "You're asking furniture what it wants to eat? Why not just upholster me?" When they stared at him, he weakened and said, "Just some Russian dressing."

Cloquet had always been an atheist, but when the priest, Father Bernard, arrived, he asked if there was still time for him to convert.

Father Bernard shook his head. "This time of year, I think most of your major faiths are filled," he said. "Probably the best I could do on such short notice is maybe make a call and get you into something Hindu. I'll need a passport-sized photograph, though."

No use, Cloquet reflected. I will have to meet my fate alone. There is no God. There is no purpose to life. Nothing lasts. Even the works of the great Shakespeare will disappear when the universe burns out—not such a terrible thought, of course, when it comes to a play like *Titus Andronicus*, but what about the others? No wonder some people commit suicide! Why not end this absurdity? Why go through with this hollow charade called life? Why, except that somewhere within us a voice says, "Live." Always, from some inner region, we hear the command, "Keep living!" Cloquet recognized the voice; it was his insurance salesman. Naturally, he thought—Fishbein doesn't want to pay off.

Cloquet longed to be free—to be out of jail, skipping through an open meadow. (Cloquet always skipped when he was happy. Indeed, the habit had kept him out of the Army.) The thought of freedom made him feel simultaneously exhilarated and terrified. If I were truly free, he thought, I could exercise my possibilities to the fullest. Perhaps I could become a ventriloquist, as I have always wanted. Or show up at the Louvre in bikini underwear, with a fake nose and glasses.

He grew dizzy as he contemplated his choices and was about to faint, when a jailer opened his cell door and told him that the real murderer of Brisseau had just confessed. Cloquet was free to go. Cloquet sank to his knees and kissed the floor of his cell. He sang the "Marseillaise." He wept! He danced! Three days later, he was back in jail for showing up at the Louvre in bikini underwear, with a fake nose and glasses.

By Destiny Denied

(Notes for an eight-hundred-page novel—the big book they're all waiting for)

BACKGROUND—SCOTLAND, 1823:

A man has been arrested for stealing a crust of bread. "I only like the crust," he explains, and he is identified as the thief who has recently terrorized several chophouses by stealing just the end cut of roast beef. The culprit, Solomon Entwhistle, is hauled into court, and a stern judge sentences him to from five to ten years (whichever comes first) at hard labor. Entwhistle is locked in a dungeon, and in an early act of enlightened penology the key is thrown away. Despondent but determined, Entwhistle begins the arduous task of tunnelling to freedom. Meticulously digging with a spoon, he tunnels beneath the prison walls, then continues, spoonful by spoonful, under Glasgow to London. He pauses to emerge at Liverpool, but finds that he prefers the tunnel. Once in London, he stows away aboard a

25

freighter bound for the New World, where he dreams of starting life over, this time as a frog.

Arriving at Boston, Entwhistle meets Margaret Figg, a comely New England schoolteacher whose specialty is baking bread and then placing it on her head. Enticed, Entwhistle marries her, and the two open a small store, trading pelts and whale blubber for scrimshaw in an ever-increasing cycle of meaningless activity. The store is an instant success, and by 1850 Entwhistle is wealthy, educated, respected, and cheating on his wife with a large possum. He has two sons by Margaret Figg—one normal, the other simpleminded, though it is hard to tell the difference unless someone hands them each a yo-yo. His small trading post will go on to become a giant modern department store, and when he dies at eighty-five, from a combination of smallpox and a tomahawk in the skull, he is happy.

(Note: Remember to make Entwhistle likable.)

Locale and observations, 1976:

Walking east on Alton Avenue, one passes the Costello Brothers Warehouse, Adelman's Tallis Repair Shop, the Chones Funeral Parlor, and Higby's Poolroom. John Higby, the owner, is a stubby man with bushy hair who fell off a ladder at the age of nine and requires two days' advance notice to stop grinning. Turning north, or "uptown," from Higby's (actually, it is downtown, and the real uptown is now located crosstown), one comes to a small green park. Here citizens stroll and chat, and though the place is free of muggings and rapes, one is frequently accosted by panhandlers or men claiming to know Julius Caesar. Now the cool autumn breeze (known here as the santana, since it comes every year at the same time and blows most of the older population out of their shoes) causes the last leaves of summer to fall and drift into dead heaps. One is struck by an almost existential feeling of purposelessness—particularly since the massage parlors closed. There is a definite sense of metaphysical "otherness," which cannot be explained except to say it's nothing like what usually goes on in Pittsburgh. The town in its way is a metaphor, but for what? Not only is it a metaphor, it's a simile. It's "where it's at." It's "now." It's also "later." It's every town in America and it's no town. This causes great confusion among the mailmen. And the big department store is Entwhistle's.

Blanche (Base her on Cousin Tina):
Blanche Mandelstam, sweet but beefy, with nervous, pudgy fingers and thick-lensed glasses ("I wanted to be an Olympic swimmer," she told her doctor, "but I had some problems with buoyancy"), awakens to her clock radio.

Years ago, Blanche would have been considered pretty, though not later than the Pleistocene epoch. To her husband, Leon, however, she is "the most beautiful creature in the world, except for Ernest Borgnine." Blanche and Leon met long ago, at a high-school dance. (She is an excellent dancer, although during the tango she constantly consults a diagram she carries of some feet.) They talked freely and found they enjoyed many things in common. For example, both enjoyed sleeping on bacon bits. Blanche was impressed with the way Leon dressed, for she had never seen anyone wear three hats simultaneously. The couple were married, and it was not long before they had their first and only sexual experience. "It was totally sublime," Blanche recalls, "although I do remember Leon attempting to slash his wrists."

Blanche told her new husband that although he made a reasonable living as a human guinea pig, she wanted to keep her job in the shoe department of Entwhistle's. Too proud to be supported, Leon reluctantly agreed, but insisted that when she reached the age of ninety-five she must retire. Now the couple sat down to breakfast. For him, it was juice, toast, and coffee. For Blanche, the usual—a glass of hot water, a chicken wing, sweet-and-pungent pork, and cannelloni. Then she left for Entwhistle's.

(Note: Blanche should go around singing, the way Cousin Tina does, though not always the Japanese national anthem.)

Carmen (A study in psychopathology based on traits observed in Fred Simdong, his brother Lee, and their cat Sparky):

By Destiny Denied

Carmen Pinchuck, squat and bald, emerged from a steaming shower and removed his shower cap. Although totally without hair, he detested getting his scalp wet. "Why should I?" he told friends. "Then my enemies would have the advantage over me." Someone suggested that this attitude might be considered strange, but he laughed, and then, his eyes tensely darting around the room to see if he was being watched, he kissed some throw pillows. Pinchuck is a nervous man who fishes in his spare time but has not caught anything since 1923. "I guess it's not in the cards," he chortles. But when an acquaintance pointed out that he was casting his line into a jar of sweet cream he grew uneasy.

Pinchuck has done many things. He was expelled from high school for moaning in class, and has since worked as a shepherd, psychotherapist, and mime. He is currently employed by the Fish and Wildlife Service, where he is paid to teach Spanish to squirrels. Pinchuck has been described by those who love him as "a punk, a loner, a psychopath, and apple-cheeked." "He likes to sit in his room and talk back to the radio," one neighbor said. "He can be very loyal," another remarked. "Once when Mrs. Monroe slipped on the ice, he slipped on some ice out of sympathy." Politically, Pinchuck is, by his own admission, an independent, and in the last Presidential election his write-in vote was for Cesar Romero.

Now, donning his tweed hackie's cap and lifting a box wrapped in brown paper, Pinchuck left his rooming house for the street. Then, realizing he was naked except for his tweed hackie's cap, he returned, dressed, and set out for Entwhistle's.

(Note: Remember to go into greater detail about Pinchuck's hostility toward his cap.)

The Meeting (rough):

The doors to the department store opened at ten sharp, and although Monday was generally a slow day, a sale on radioactive tuna fish quickly jammed the basement. An air of imminent apocalypse hung over the shoe department like a wet tarpaulin as Carmen Pinchuck handed his box to Blanche Mandelstam and said, "I'd like to return these loafers. They're too small."

"Do you have a sales slip?" Blanche countered, trying to remain poised, although she confessed later that her world had suddenly begun falling apart. ("I can't deal with people since the accident," she has told friends. Six months ago, while playing tennis, she swallowed one of the balls. Since then her breathing has become irregular.)

"Er, no," Pinchuck replied nervously. "I lost it." (The central problem of his life is that he is always misplacing things. Once he went to sleep and when he awoke his bed was missing.) Now, as customers lined up behind him impatiently, he broke into a cold sweat.

"You'll have to have it O.K.'d by the floor manager," Blanche said, referring Pinchuck to Mr. Dubinsky, whom she had been having an affair with since Halloween. (Lou Dubinsky, a graduate of the best typing school in Europe, was a genius until alcohol reduced his speed to one word per day and he was forced to go to work in a department store.)

"Have you worn them?" Blanche continued, fighting back tears. The notion of Pinchuck in his loafers was unbearable to her. "My father used to wear loafers," she confessed. "Both on the same foot."

Pinchuck was writhing now. "No," he said. "Er—I mean yes. I had them on briefly, but only while I took a bath."

"Why did you buy them if they're too small?" Blanche asked, unaware that she was articulating a quintessential human paradox.

The truth was that Pinchuck had not felt comfortable in the shoes but he could never bring himself to say no to a salesman. "I want to be *liked*," he admitted to Blanche. "Once I bought a live wildebeest because I couldn't say no." (Note: O. F. Krumgold has written a brilliant paper about certain tribes in Borneo that do not have a word for "no" in their language and consequently turn down requests by nodding their heads and saying, "I'll get back to you." This corroborates his earlier theories that the urge to be liked at any cost is not socially adaptive but genetic, much the same as the ability to sit through operetta.)

By eleven-ten, the floor manager, Dubinsky, had O.K.'d the exchange, and Pinchuck was given a larger pair of shoes. Pinchuck confessed later that the incident had caused him to experience severe depression and wooziness, which he also attributed to the news of his parrot's wedding.

Shortly after the Entwhistle affair, Carmen Pinchuck quit his job and became a Chinese waiter at the Sung Ching Cantonese Palace. Blanche Mandelstam then suffered a major nervous breakdown and tried to elope with a photograph of Dizzy Dean. (Note: Upon reflection, perhaps it would be best to make Dubinsky a hand puppet.) Late in January, Entwhistle's closed its doors for the last time, and Julie Entwhistle, the owner, took his family, whom he loved very dearly, and moved them into the Bronx Zoo.

(This last sentence should remain intact. It seems very very great. End of Chapter 1 notes.)

The UFO Menace

UFOS ARE BACK in the news, and it is high time we took a serious look at this phenomenon. (Actually, the time is ten past eight, so not only are we a few minutes late but I'm hungry.) Up until now, the entire subject of flying saucers has been mostly associated with kooks or oddballs. Frequently, in fact, observers will admit to being a member of both groups. Still, persistent sightings by responsible individuals have caused the Air Force and the scientific community to reexamine a once skeptical attitude, and the sum of two hundred dollars has now been allocated for a comprehensive study of the phenomenon. The question is: Is anything out there? And if so, do they have ray guns?

All UFOs may not prove to be of extraterrestrial origin, but experts do agree that any glowing cigar-shaped aircraft capable of rising straight up at twelve thousand miles per second would require the kind of maintenance and sparkplugs available only on Pluto. If these objects are indeed from another planet, then the civilization that designed them must be millions of years more advanced than our own. Either that or they are very lucky. Professor Leon Speciman postulates a civilization in outer space that is more advanced than ours by approximately fifteen minutes. This, he feels, gives them a great advantage over us, since they needn't rush to get to appointments.

Dr. Brackish Menzies, who works at the Mount Wilson Observatory, or else is under observation at the Mount Wilson Mental Hospital (the letter is not clear), claims that travellers moving at close to the speed of light would require many millions of years to get here, even from the nearest solar system, and, judging from the shows on Broadway, the trip would hardly be worth it. (It is impossible to travel faster than light, and certainly not desirable, as one's hat keeps blowing off.)

Interestingly, according to modern astronomers, space is finite. This is a very comforting thought—particularly for people who can never remember where they have left things. The key factor in thinking about the universe, however, is that it is expanding and will one day break apart and disappear. That is why if the girl in the office down the hall has some good points but perhaps not all the qualities you require it's best to compromise.

The most frequently asked question about the

UFOs is: If saucers come from outer space, why have their pilots not attempted to make contact with us, instead of hovering mysteriously over deserted areas? My own theory is that for creatures from another solar system "hovering" may be a socially acceptable mode of relating. It may, indeed, be pleasurable. I myself once hovered over an eighteen-year-old actress for six months and had the best time of my life. It should also be recalled that when we talk of "life" on other planets we are frequently referring to amino acids, which are never very gregarious, even at parties.

Most people tend to think of UFOs as a modern problem, but could they be a phenomenon that man has been aware of for centuries? (To us a century seems quite long, particularly if you are holding an I.O.U., but by astronomical standards it is over in a second. For that reason, it is always best to carry a toothbrush and be ready to leave on a moment's notice.) Scholars now tell us that the sighting of unidentified flying objects dates as far back as Biblical times. For instance, there is a passage in the Book of Leviticus that reads, "And a great and silver ball appeared over the Assyrian Armies, and in all of Babylonia there was wailing and gnashing of teeth, till the Prophets bade the multitudes get a grip on themselves and shape up."

Was this phenomenon related to one described years later by Parmenides: "Three orange objects did appear suddenly in the heavens and did circle midtown Athens, hovering over the baths and causing several of our wisest philosophers to grab for towels"? And, again, were those "orange objects" similar to what is described in a recently discovered twelfth-century Saxon-church manuscript: "A lauch lauched he; wer richt laith to weet a cork-heild schonne; whilst a red balle lang owre swam aboone. I thank you, ladies and gentlemen"?

This last account was taken by medieval clergy to signify that the world was coming to an end, and there was great disappointment when Monday came and everyone had to go back to work.

Finally, and most convincingly, in 1822 Goethe himself notes a strange celestial phenomenon. "En route home from the Leipzig Anxiety Festival," he wrote, "I was crossing a meadow, when I chanced to look up and saw several fiery red balls suddenly appear in the southern sky. They descended at a great rate of speed and began chasing me. I screamed that I was a genius and consequently could not run very fast, but my words were wasted. I became enraged and shouted imprecations at them, whereupon they flew away frightened. I related this story to Beethoven, not realizing he had already gone deaf, and he smiled and nodded and said, 'Right.' "

As a general rule, careful on-the-scene investigations disclose that most "unidentified" flying objects are quite ordinary phenomena, such as weather balloons, meteorites, satellites, and even once a man named Lewis Mandelbaum, who blew off the roof of the World Trade Center. A typical "explained" incident is the one reported by Sir Chester Ramsbottom, on June 5, 1961, in Shropshire: "I was driving along the road at 2 A.M. and saw a cigar-shaped object that seemed to be tracking my car. No matter which way I drove, it stayed with me, turning sharply at right angles. It was a fierce, glowing red, and in spite of twisting and turning the car at high speed I could not lose it. I became alarmed and began sweating. I let out a shriek of terror and apparently fainted, but awoke in a hospital, miraculously unharmed." Upon investigation, experts determined that the "cigar-shaped object" was Sir Chester's nose. Naturally, all his evasive actions could not lose it, since it was attached to his face.

Another explained incident began in late April of 1972, with a report from Major General Curtis Memling, of Andrews Air Force Base: "I was walking across a field one night and suddenly I saw a large silver disc in the sky. It flew over me, not fifty feet above my head, and repeatedly described aerodynamic patterns impossible for any normal aircraft. Suddenly it accelerated and shot away at terrific speed."

Investigators became suspicious when they noticed that General Memling could not describe this incident without giggling. He later admitted he had just come from a showing of the film "War of the Worlds," at the post movie theatre, and "got a very big kick out of it." Ironically, General Memling reported another UFO sighting in

1976, but it was soon discovered that he, too, had become fixated on Sir Chester Ramsbottom's nose—an occurrence that caused consternation in the Air Force and eventually led to General Memling's court-martial.

If most UFO sightings can be satisfactorily explained, what of those few which cannot? Following are some of the most mystifying examples of "unsolved" encounters, the first reported by a Boston man in May, 1969: "I was walking by the beach with my wife. She's not a very attractive woman. Rather overweight. In fact, I was pulling her on a dolly at the time. Suddenly I looked up and saw a huge white saucer that seemed to be descending at great speed. I guess I panicked, because I dropped the rope on my wife's dolly and began running. The saucer passed directly over my head and I heard an eerie, metallic voice say, 'Call your service.' When I got home, I phoned my answering service and received a message that my brother Ralph had moved and to forward all his mail to Neptune. I never saw him again. My wife suffered a severe breakdown over the incident and now cannot converse without using a hand puppet."

From I. M. Axelbank, of Athens, Georgia, February, 1971: "I am an experienced pilot and was flying my private Cessna from New Mexico to Amarillo, Texas, to bomb some people whose religious persuasion I do not wholly agree with, when I noticed an object flying alongside me. At first I thought it was another plane, until it emitted a green beam of light, forcing my plane to drop eleven thousand feet in four seconds and causing my toupee to snap off my head and tear a two-foot hole in the roof. I repeatedly called for help on my radio, but for some reason could only get the old 'Mr. Anthony' program. The UFO came very close to my plane again and then shot away at blinding speed. By this time I had lost my bearings and was forced to make an emergency landing on the turnpike. I continued the trip in the plane on the ground and only got into trouble when I tried to run a toll booth and broke off my wings."

One of the eeriest accounts occurred in August, 1975, to a man on Montauk Point, in Long Island: "I was in bed at my beach house, but could not sleep because of some fried chicken in the icebox that I felt entitled to. I waited till my wife dropped off, and tiptoed into the kitchen. I remember looking at the clock. It was precisely four-fifteen. I'm quite certain of this, because our kitchen clock has not worked in twenty-one years and is always at that time. I also noticed that our dog, Judas, was acting funny. He was standing up on his hind legs and singing, 'I Enjoy Being a Girl.' Suddenly the room turned bright orange. At first, I thought my wife had caught me eating between meals and set fire to the house. Then I looked out the window, where to my amazement I saw a gigantic cigar-shaped aircraft hovering just over the treetops in the yard and emitting an orange glow. I stood transfixed for what must

41

have been several hours, though our clock still read four-fifteen, so it was difficult to tell. Finally, a large, mechanical claw extended from the aircraft and snatched the two pieces of chicken from my hand and quickly retreated. The machine then rose and, accelerating at great speed, vanished into the sky. When I reported the incident to the Air Force, they told me that what I had seen was a flock of birds. When I protested, Colonel Quincy Bascomb personally promised that the Air Force would return the two pieces of chicken. To this day, I have only received one piece."

Finally, an account in January, 1977, by two Louisiana factory workers: "Roy and I was catfishing in the bog. I enjoy the bog, as does Roy. We was not drinking, although we had brought with us a gallon of methyl chloride, which we both favor with either a twist of lemon or a small onion. Anyways, at about midnight we looked up and saw a bright-yellow sphere descend into the bog. At first Roy mistook it for a whooping crane and took a shot at it, but I said, 'Roy, that ain't no crane, 'cause it's got no beak.' That's how you can tell a crane. Roy's son Gus has a beak, you know, and thinks he's a crane. Anyways, all of a sudden this door slides open and several creatures emerge. These creatures looked like little portable radios with teeth and short hair. They also had legs, although where the toes usually are they had wheels. The creatures motioned to me to come forward, which I did, and they injected me with a fluid that caused me to smile and act like Bopeep. They spoke with one another in a strange tongue, which sounded like when you back your car over a fat person. They took me aboard the aircraft and gave me what seemed to be a complete physical examination. I went along with it, as I had not had a checkup in two years. By now they had mastered my own language, but they still made simple mistakes like using 'hermeneutics,' when they meant 'heuristic.' They told me they were from another galaxy and were here to tell the earth that we must learn to live in peace or they will return with special weapons and laminate every first-born male. They said they would get the results of my blood test back in a couple of days and if I didn't hear from them I could go ahead and marry Clair."

My Apology

OF ALL THE famous men who ever lived, the one I would most like to have been was Socrates. Not just because he was a great thinker, because I have been known to have some reasonably profound insights myself, although mine invariably revolve around a Swedish airline stewardess and some handcuffs. No, the great appeal for me of this wisest of all Greeks was his courage in the face of death. His decision was not to abandon his principles, but rather to give his life to prove a point. I personally am not quite as fearless about dying and will, after any untoward noise such as a car backfiring, leap directly into the arms of the person I am conversing with. In the end, Socrates' brave death gave his life authentic meaning; something my existence lacks totally, although it does possess a minimal relevance to the Internal Revenue Department. I must confess I have tried putting myself in this great philosopher's sandals many times and no matter how often I do, I immediately wind up dozing off and having the following dream.

(The scene is my prison cell. I am usually sitting alone, working out some deep problem of rational thought like: Can an object be called a work of art if it can also be used to clean the stove? Presently I am visited by Agathon and Simmias.)

Agathon: Ah, my good friend and wise old sage. How go your days of confinement?

Allen: What can one say of confinement, Agathon? Only the body may be circumscribed. My mind roams freely, unfettered by the four walls and therefore in truth I ask, does confinement exist?

Agathon: Well, what if you want to take a walk?

Allen: Good question. I can't.

(The three of us sit in classical poses, not unlike a frieze. Finally Agathon speaks.)

Agathon: I'm afraid the word is bad. You have been condemned to death.

Allen: Ah, it saddens me that I should cause debate in the senate.

48

My Apology

Agathon: No debate. Unanimous.

Allen: Really?

Agathon: First ballot.

Allen: Hmmm. I had counted on a little more support.

Simmias: The senate is furious over your ideas for a Utopian state.

Allen: I guess I should never have suggested having a philosopher-king.

Simmias: Especially when you kept pointing to yourself and clearing your throat.

Allen: And yet I do not regard my executioners as evil.

Agathon: Nor do I.

Allen: Er, yeah, well . . . for what is evil but merely good in excess?

Agathon: How so?

Allen: Look at it this way. If a man sings a lovely song it is beautiful. If he keeps singing, one begins to get a headache.

Agathon: True.

Allen: And if he definitely won't stop singing, eventually you want to stuff socks down his throat.

Agathon: Yes. Very true.

Allen: When is the sentence to be carried out?

Agathon: What time is it now?

Allen: Today!?

Agathon: They need the jail cell.

Allen: Then let it be! Let them take my life. Let it be recorded that I died rather than abandon the principles of truth and free inquiry. Weep not, Agathon.

Agathon: I'm not weeping. This is an allergy.

Allen: For to the man of the mind, death is not an end but a beginning.

Simmias: How so?

Allen: Well, now give me a minute.

Simmias: Take your time.

Allen: It is true, Simmias, that man does not exist before he is born, is it not?

Simmias: Very true.

Allen: Nor does he exist after his death.

Simmias: Yes. I agree.

Allen: Hmmm.

Simmias: So?

Allen: Now, wait a minute. I'm a little confused. You know they only feed me lamb and it's never well-cooked.

Simmias: Most men regard death as the final end. Consequently they fear it.

Allen: Death is a state of non-being. That which is not, does not exist. Therefore death does not exist. Only truth exists. Truth and beauty. Each is interchangeable, but are aspects of themselves. Er, what specifically did they say they had in mind for me?

Agathon: Hemlock.

Allen: (Puzzled) Hemlock?

Agathon: You remember that black liquid that ate through your marble table?

Allen: Really?

Agathon: Just one cupful. Though they do have a back-up chalice should you spill anything.

Allen: I wonder if it's painful?

Agathon: They asked if you would try not to make a scene. It disturbs the other prisoners.

Allen: Hmmm . . .

Agathon: I told everyone you would die bravely rather than renounce your principles.

Allen: Right, right . . . er, did the concept of "exile" ever come up?

Agathon: They stopped exiling last year. Too much red tape.

Allen: Right . . . yeah . . . (*Troubled and distracted but trying to remain self-possessed*) I er . . . so er . . . so—what else is new?

Agathon: Oh, I ran into Isosceles. He has a great idea for a new triangle.

Allen: Right . . . right . . . *(Suddenly dropping all pretense of courage)* Look, I'm going to level with you—I don't want to go! I'm too young!

Agathon: But this is your chance to die for truth!

Allen: Don't misunderstand me. I'm all for truth. On the other hand I have a lunch date in Sparta next week and I'd hate to miss it. It's my turn to buy. You know those Spartans, they fight so easily.

Simmias: Is our wisest philosopher a coward?

Allen: I'm not a coward, and I'm not a hero. I'm somewhere in the middle.

Simmias: A cringing vermin.

Allen: That's approximately the spot.

Agathon: But it was you who proved that death doesn't exist.

Allen: Hey, listen—I've proved a lot of things. That's how I pay my rent. Theories and little observations. A puckish remark now and then. Occasional maxims. It beats picking olives, but let's not get carried away.

Agathon: But you have proved many times that the soul is immortal.

Allen: And it is! On paper. See, that's the thing about philosophy—it's not all that functional once you get out of class.

Simmias: And the eternal "forms"? You said each thing always did exist and always will exist.

Allen: I was talking mostly about heavy objects. A statue or something. With people it's a lot different.

Agathon: But all that talk about death being the same as sleep.

Allen: Yes, but the difference is that when you're dead and somebody yells, "Everybody up, it's morning," it's very hard to find your slippers.

(The executioner arrives with a cup of hemlock. He bears a close facial resemblance to the Irish comedian Spike Milligan.)

Executioner: Ah—here we are. Who gets the poison?

Agathon: (Pointing to me) He does.

Allen: Gee, it's a big cup. Should it be smoking like that?

Executioner: Yes. And drink it all because a lot of times the poison's at the bottom.

Allen: (Usually here my behavior is totally different from Socrates' and I am told I scream in my sleep.) No—I won't! I don't want to die! Help! No! Please!

(He hands me the bubbling brew amidst my disgusting pleading and all seems lost. Then because of some innate survival instinct the dream always takes an upturn and a messenger arrives.)

Messenger: Hold everything! The senate has revoted! The charges are dropped. Your value has been reassessed and it is decided you should be honored instead.

Allen: At last! At last! They came to their senses! I'm a free man! Free! And to be honored yet! Quick, Agathon and Simmias, get my bags. I must be going. Praxiteles will want to get an early start on my bust. But before I leave, I give a little parable.

Simmias: Gee, that really was a sharp reversal. I wonder if they know what they're doing?

Allen: A group of men live in a dark cave. They are unaware that outside the sun shines. The only light they know is the flickering flame of a few small candles which they use to move around.

Agathon: Where'd they get the candles?

Allen: Well, let's just say they have them.

Agathon: They live in a cave and have candles? It doesn't ring true.

Allen: Can't you just buy it for now?

Agathon: O.K., O.K., but get to the point.

Allen: And then one day, one of the cave dwellers wanders out of the cave and sees the outside world.

Simmias: In all its clarity.

Allen: Precisely. In all its clarity.

Agathon: When he tries to tell the others they don't believe him.

Allen: Well, no. He doesn't tell the others.

Agathon: He doesn't?

Allen: No, he opens a meat market, he marries a dancer and dies of a cerebral hemorrhage at forty-two.

(They grab me and force the hemlock down. Here I usually wake up in a sweat and only some eggs and smoked salmon calm me down.)

The Kugelmass
Episode

KUGELMASS, A PROFESSOR of humanities at City College, was unhappily married for the second time. Daphne Kugelmass was an oaf. He also had two dull sons by his first wife, Flo, and was up to his neck in alimony and child support.

"Did I know it would turn out so badly?" Kugelmass whined to his analyst one day. "Daphne had promise. Who suspected she'd let herself go and swell up like a beach ball? Plus she had a few bucks, which is not in itself a healthy reason to marry a person, but it doesn't hurt, with the kind of operating nut I have. You see my point?"

Kugelmass was bald and as hairy as a bear, but he had soul.

"I need to meet a new woman," he went on. "I need to have an affair. I may not look the part, but I'm a man who needs romance. I need softness, I need flirtation. I'm not getting younger, so before it's too late I want to make love in Venice, trade quips at '21,' and exchange coy glances over red wine and candlelight. You see what I'm saying?"

Dr. Mandel shifted in his chair and said, "An affair will solve nothing. You're so unrealistic. Your problems run much deeper."

"And also this affair must be discreet," Kugelmass continued. "I can't afford a second divorce. Daphne would really sock it to me."

"Mr. Kugelmass—"

"But it can't be anyone at City College, because Daphne also works there. Not that anyone on the faculty at C.C.N.Y. is any great shakes, but some of those coeds . . ."

"Mr. Kugelmass—"

"Help me. I had a dream last night. I was skipping through a meadow holding a picnic basket and the basket was marked 'Options.' And then I saw there was a hole in the basket."

"Mr. Kugelmass, the worst thing you could do is act out. You must simply express your feelings here, and together we'll analyze them. You have been in treatment long enough to know there is no overnight cure. After all, I'm an analyst, not a magician."

"Then perhaps what I need is a magician," Kugelmass said, rising from his chair. And with that he terminated his therapy.

A couple of weeks later, while Kugelmass and Daphne were moping around in their apartment one night like two pieces of old furniture, the phone rang.

"I'll get it," Kugelmass said. "Hello."

"Kugelmass?" a voice said. "Kugelmass, this is Persky."

"Who?"

"Persky. Or should I say The Great Persky?"

"Pardon me?"

"I hear you're looking all over town for a magician to bring a little exotica into your life? Yes or no?"

"Sh-h-h," Kugelmass whispered. "Don't hang up. Where are you calling from, Persky?"

Early the following afternoon, Kugelmass climbed three flights of stairs in a broken-down apartment house in the Bushwick section of Brooklyn. Peering through the darkness of the hall, he found the door he was looking for and pressed the bell. I'm going to regret this, he thought to himself.

Seconds later, he was greeted by a short, thin, waxy-looking man.

"*You're* Persky the Great?" Kugelmass said.

"The Great Persky. You want a tea?"

"No, I want romance. I want music. I want love and beauty."

"But not tea, eh? Amazing. O.K., sit down."

Persky went to the back room, and Kugelmass heard the sounds of boxes and furniture being moved around. Persky reappeared, pushing before him a large object on squeaky roller-skate wheels. He removed some old silk handkerchiefs

that were lying on its top and blew away a bit
of dust. It was a cheap-looking Chinese cabinet,
badly lacquered.

"Persky," Kugelmass said, "what's your scam?"

"Pay attention," Persky said. "This is some
beautiful effect. I developed it for a Knights of
Pythias date last year, but the booking fell
through. Get into the cabinet."

"Why, so you can stick it full of swords or
something?"

"You see any swords?"

Kugelmass made a face and, grunting, climbed
into the cabinet. He couldn't help noticing a
couple of ugly rhinestones glued onto the raw
plywood just in front of his face. "If this is a
joke," he said.

"Some joke. Now, here's the point. If I throw
any novel into this cabinet with you, shut the
doors, and tap it three times, you will find yourself projected into that book."

Kugelmass made a grimace of disbelief.

"It's the emess," Persky said. "My hand to
God. Not just a novel, either. A short story, a
play, a poem. You can meet any of the women
created by the world's best writers. Whoever you
dreamed of. You could carry on all you like with
a real winner. Then when you've had enough you
give a yell, and I'll see you're back here in a
split second."

"Persky, are you some kind of outpatient?"

"I'm telling you it's on the level," Persky said.
Kugelmass remained skeptical. "What are you

telling me—that this cheesy homemade box can take me on a ride like you're describing?"

"For a double sawbuck."

Kugelmass reached for his wallet. "I'll believe this when I see it," he said.

Persky tucked the bills in his pants pocket and turned toward his bookcase. "So who do you want to meet? Sister Carrie? Hester Prynne? Ophelia? Maybe someone by Saul Bellow? Hey, what about Temple Drake? Although for a man your age she'd be a workout."

"French. I want to have an affair with a French lover."

"Nana?"

"I don't want to have to pay for it."

"What about Natasha in *War and Peace?*"

"I said French. I know! What about Emma Bovary? That sounds to me perfect."

"You got it, Kugelmass. Give me a holler when you've had enough." Persky tossed in a paperback copy of Flaubert's novel.

"You sure this is safe?" Kugelmass asked as Persky began shutting the cabinet doors.

"Safe. Is anything safe in this crazy world?" Persky rapped three times on the cabinet and then flung open the doors.

Kugelmass was gone. At the same moment, he appeared in the bedroom of Charles and Emma Bovary's house at Yonville. Before him was a beautiful woman, standing alone with her back turned to him as she folded some linen. I can't believe this, thought Kugelmass, staring at the doctor's ravishing wife. This is uncanny. I'm here. It's her.

Emma turned in surprise. "Goodness, you startled me," she said. "Who are you?" She spoke in the same fine English translation as the paperback.

It's simply devastating, he thought. Then, realizing that it was he whom she had addressed, he said, "Excuse me. I'm Sidney Kugelmass. I'm from City College. A professor of humanities. C.C.N.Y.? Uptown. I—oh, boy!"

Emma Bovary smiled flirtatiously and said, "Would you like a drink? A glass of wine, perhaps?"

She is beautiful, Kugelmass thought. What a contrast with the troglodyte who shared his bed! He felt a sudden impulse to take this vision into his arms and tell her she was the kind of woman he had dreamed of all his life.

"Yes, some wine," he said hoarsely. "White. No, red. No, white. Make it white."

"Charles is out for the day," Emma said, her voice full of playful implication.

After the wine, they went for a stroll in the lovely French countryside. "I've always dreamed that some mysterious stranger would appear and rescue me from the monotony of this crass rural existence," Emma said, clasping his hand. They passed a small church. "I love what you have on," she murmured. "I've never seen anything like it around here. It's so . . . so modern."

"It's called a leisure suit," he said romantically. "It was marked down." Suddenly he kissed her. For the next hour they reclined under a tree and whispered together and told each other deeply meaningful things with their eyes. Then Kugelmass sat up. He had just remembered he had to meet Daphne at Bloomingdale's. "I must go," he told her. "But don't worry, I'll be back."

"I hope so," Emma said.

He embraced her passionately, and the two walked back to the house. He held Emma's face cupped in his palms, kissed her again, and yelled, "O.K., Persky! I got to be at Bloomingdale's by three-thirty."

There was an audible pop, and Kugelmass was back in Brooklyn.

"So? Did I lie?" Persky asked triumphantly.

"Look, Persky, I'm right now late to meet the ball and chain at Lexington Avenue, but when can I go again? Tomorrow?"

"My pleasure. Just bring a twenty. And don't mention this to anybody."

"Yeah. I'm going to call Rupert Murdoch."

Kugelmass hailed a cab and sped off to the city. His heart danced on point. I am in love, he thought, I am the possessor of a wonderful secret. What he didn't realize was that at this very moment students in various classrooms across the country were saying to their teachers, "Who is this character on page 100? A bald Jew is kissing Madame Bovary?" A teacher in Sioux Falls, South Dakota, sighed and thought, Jesus, these kids, with their pot and acid. What goes through their minds!

Daphne Kugelmass was in the bathroom-accessories department at Bloomingdale's when Kugelmass arrived breathlessly. "Where've you been?" she snapped. "It's four-thirty."

"I got held up in traffic," Kugelmass said.

Kugelmass visited Persky the next day, and in a few minutes was again passed magically to Yonville. Emma couldn't hide her excitement at seeing him. The two spent hours together, laughing and talking about their different backgrounds. Before Kugelmass left, they made love. "My God, I'm doing it with Madame Bovary!" Kugelmass whispered to himself. "Me, who failed freshman English."

As the months passed, Kugelmass saw Persky many times and developed a close and passionate relationship with Emma Bovary. "Make sure and always get me into the book before page 120," Kugelmass said to the magician one day. "I always have to meet her before she hooks up with this Rodolphe character."

"Why?" Persky asked. "You can't beat his time?"

"Beat his time. He's landed gentry. Those guys have nothing better to do than flirt and ride horses. To me, he's one of those faces you see in the pages of *Women's Wear Daily*. With the Helmut Berger hairdo. But to her he's hot stuff."

"And her husband suspects nothing?"

"He's out of his depth. He's a lacklustre little paramedic who's thrown in his lot with a jitterbug. He's ready to go to sleep by ten, and she's putting on her dancing shoes. Oh, well . . . See you later."

And once again Kugelmass entered the cabinet and passed instantly to the Bovary estate at Yonville. "How you doing, cupcake?" he said to Emma.

"Oh, Kugelmass," Emma sighed. "What I have to put up with. Last night at dinner, Mr. Personality dropped off to sleep in the middle of the dessert course. I'm pouring my heart out about Maxim's and the ballet, and out of the blue I hear snoring."

"It's O.K., darling. I'm here now," Kugelmass said, embracing her. I've earned this, he thought, smelling Emma's French perfume and burying his nose in her hair. I've suffered enough. I've paid enough analysts. I've searched till I'm weary. She's young and nubile, and I'm here a few pages after Leon and just before Rodolphe. By showing up during the correct chapters, I've got the situation knocked.

Emma, to be sure, was just as happy as Kugelmass. She had been starved for excitement, and his tales of Broadway night life, of fast cars and Hollywood and TV stars, enthralled the young French beauty.

"Tell me again about O. J. Simpson," she implored that evening, as she and Kugelmass strolled past Abbé Bournisien's church.

"What can I say? The man is great. He sets all kinds of rushing records. Such moves. They can't touch him."

"And the Academy Awards?" Emma said wistfully. "I'd give anything to win one."

"First you've got to be nominated."

"I know. You explained it. But I'm convinced I can act. Of course, I'd want to take a class or two. With Strasberg maybe. Then, if I had the right agent—"

"We'll see, we'll see. I'll speak to Persky."

That night, safely returned to Persky's flat, Kugelmass brought up the idea of having Emma visit him in the big city.

"Let me think about it," Persky said. "Maybe I could work it. Stranger things have happened." Of course, neither of them could think of one.

"Where the hell do you go all the time?" Daphne Kugelmass barked at her husband as he returned home late that evening. "You got a chippie stashed somewhere?"

"Yeah, sure, I'm just the type," Kugelmass said wearily. "I was with Leonard Popkin. We were discussing Socialist agriculture in Poland. You know Popkin. He's a freak on the subject."

"Well, you've been very odd lately," Daphne said. "Distant. Just don't forget about my father's birthday. On Saturday?"

"Oh, sure, sure," Kugelmass said, heading for the bathroom.

"My whole family will be there. We can see

the twins. And Cousin Hamish. You should be more polite to Cousin Hamish—he likes you."

"Right, the twins," Kugelmass said, closing the bathroom door and shutting out the sound of his wife's voice. He leaned against it and took a deep breath. In a few hours, he told himself, he would be back in Yonville again, back with his beloved. And this time, if all went well, he would bring Emma back with him.

At three-fifteen the following afternoon, Persky worked his wizardry again. Kugelmass appeared before Emma, smiling and eager. The two spent a few hours at Yonville with Binet and then remounted the Bovary carriage. Following Persky's instructions, they held each other tightly, closed their eyes, and counted to ten. When they opened them, the carriage was just drawing up at the side door of the Plaza Hotel, where Kugelmass had optimistically reserved a suite earlier in the day.

"I love it! It's everything I dreamed it would be," Emma said as she swirled joyously around the bedroom, surveying the city from their window. "There's F. A. O. Schwarz. And there's Central Park, and the Sherry is which one? Oh, there—I see. It's too divine."

On the bed there were boxes from Halston and Saint Laurent. Emma unwrapped a package and held up a pair of black velvet pants against her perfect body.

"The slacks suit is by Ralph Lauren," Kugelmass said. "You'll look like a million bucks in it. Come on, sugar, give us a kiss."

"I've never been so happy!" Emma squealed as she stood before the mirror. "Let's go out on the town. I want to see *Chorus Line* and the Guggenheim and this Jack Nicholson character you always talk about. Are any of his flicks showing?"

"I cannot get my mind around this," a Stanford professor said. "First a strange character named Kugelmass, and now she's gone from the book. Well, I guess the mark of a classic is that you can reread it a thousand times and always find something new."

The lovers passed a blissful weekend. Kugelmass had told Daphne he would be away at a symposium in Boston and would return Monday. Savoring each moment, he and Emma went to the movies, had dinner in Chinatown, passed two hours at a discothèque, and went to bed with a TV movie. They slept till noon on Sunday, visited SoHo, and ogled celebrities at Elaine's. They had caviar and champagne in their suite on Sunday night and talked until dawn. That morning, in the cab taking them to Persky's apartment, Kugelmass thought, It was hectic, but worth it. I can't bring her here too often, but now and then it will be a charming contrast with Yonville.

At Persky's, Emma climbed into the cabinet, arranged her new boxes of clothes neatly around her, and kissed Kugelmass fondly. "My place next time," she said with a wink. Persky rapped three times on the cabinet. Nothing happened.

"Hmm," Persky said, scratching his head. He rapped again, but still no magic. "Something must be wrong," he mumbled.

"Persky, you're joking!" Kugelmass cried. "How can it not work?"

"Relax, relax. Are you still in the box, Emma?"

"Yes."

Persky rapped again—harder this time.

"I'm still here, Persky."

"I know, darling. Sit tight."

"Persky, we *have* to get her back," Kugelmass whispered. "I'm a married man, and I have a class in three hours. I'm not prepared for anything more than a cautious affair at this point."

"I can't understand it," Persky muttered. "It's such a reliable little trick."

But he could do nothing. "It's going to take a little while," he said to Kugelmass. "I'm going to have to strip it down. I'll call you later."

Kugelmass bundled Emma into a cab and took her back to the Plaza. He barely made it to his class on time. He was on the phone all day, to Persky and to his mistress. The magician told him it might be several days before he got to the bottom of the trouble.

"How was the symposium?" Daphne asked him that night.

"Fine, fine," he said, lighting the filter end of a cigarette.

"What's wrong? You're as tense as a cat."

"Me? Ha, that's a laugh. I'm as calm as a summer night. I'm just going to take a walk." He eased out the door, hailed a cab, and flew to the Plaza.

"This is no good," Emma said. "Charles will miss me."

"Bear with me, sugar," Kugelmass said. He was pale and sweaty. He kissed her again, raced to the elevators, yelled at Persky over a pay phone in the Plaza lobby, and just made it home before midnight.

"According to Popkin, barley prices in Kraków have not been this stable since 1971," he said to Daphne, and smiled wanly as he climbed into bed.

The whole week went by like that.

On Friday night, Kugelmass told Daphne there was another symposium he had to catch, this one in Syracuse. He hurried back to the Plaza, but the second weekend there was nothing like the first. "Get me back into the novel or marry me," Emma told Kugelmass. "Meanwhile, I want to get a job or go to class, because watching TV all day is the pits."

"Fine. We can use the money," Kugelmass said. "You consume twice your weight in room service."

"I met an Off Broadway producer in Central Park yesterday, and he said I might be right for a project he's doing," Emma said.

"Who is this clown?" Kugelmass asked.

The Kugelmass Episode

"He's not a clown. He's sensitive and kind and cute. His name's Jeff Something-or-Other, and he's up for a Tony."

Later that afternoon, Kugelmass showed up at Persky's drunk.

"Relax," Persky told him. "You'll get a coronary."

"Relax. The man says relax. I've got a fictional character stashed in a hotel room, and I think my wife is having me tailed by a private shamus."

"O.K., O.K. We know there's a problem." Persky crawled under the cabinet and started banging on something with a large wrench.

"I'm like a wild animal," Kugelmass went on. "I'm sneaking around town, and Emma and I have had it up to here with each other. Not to mention a hotel tab that reads like the defense budget."

"So what should I do? This is the world of magic," Persky said. "It's all nuance."

"Nuance, my foot. I'm pouring Dom Pérignon and black eggs into this little mouse, plus her wardrobe, plus she's enrolled at the Neighborhood Playhouse and suddenly needs professional photos. Also, Persky, Professor Fivish Kopkind, who teaches Comp Lit and who has always been jealous of me, has identified me as the sporadically appearing character in the Flaubert book. He's threatened to go to Daphne. I see ruin and alimony; jail. For adultery with Madame Bovary, my wife will reduce me to beggary."

"What do you want me to say? I'm working on

75

it night and day. As far as your personal anxiety goes, that I can't help you with. I'm a magician, not an analyst."

By Sunday afternoon, Emma had locked herself in the bathroom and refused to respond to Kugelmass's entreaties. Kugelmass stared out the window at the Wollman Rink and contemplated suicide. Too bad this is a low floor, he thought, or I'd do it right now. Maybe if I ran away to Europe and started life over . . . Maybe I could sell the *International Herald Tribune,* like those young girls used to.

The phone rang. Kugelmass lifted it to his ear mechanically.

"Bring her over," Persky said. "I think I got the bugs out of it."

Kugelmass's heart leaped. "You're serious?" he said. "You got it licked?"

"It was something in the transmission. Go figure."

"Persky, you're a genius. We'll be there in a minute. Less than a minute."

Again the lovers hurried to the magician's apartment, and again Emma Bovary climbed into the cabinet with her boxes. This time there was no kiss. Persky shut the doors, took a deep breath, and tapped the box three times. There was the reassuring popping noise, and when Persky peered inside, the box was empty. Madame Bovary was back in her novel. Kugelmass heaved a great sigh of relief and pumped the magician's hand.

"It's over," he said. "I learned my lesson. I'll never cheat again, I swear it." He pumped Persky's hand again and made a mental note to send him a necktie.

Three weeks later, at the end of a beautiful spring afternoon, Persky answered his doorbell. It was Kugelmass, with a sheepish expression on his face.

"O.K., Kugelmass," the magician said. "Where to this time?"

"It's just this once," Kugelmass said. "The weather is so lovely, and I'm not getting any younger. Listen, you've read *Portnoy's Complaint?* Remember The Monkey?"

"The price is now twenty-five dollars, because the cost of living is up, but I'll start you off with one freebie, due to all the trouble I caused you."

"You're good people," Kugelmass said, combing his few remaining hairs as he climbed into the cabinet again. "This'll work all right?"

"I hope. But I haven't tried it much since all that unpleasantness."

"Sex and romance," Kugelmass said from inside the box. "What we go through for a pretty face."

Persky tossed in a copy of *Portnoy's Complaint* and rapped three times on the box. This time, instead of a popping noise there was a dull explosion, followed by a series of crackling noises and a shower of sparks. Persky leaped back, was seized by a heart attack, and dropped dead. The cabinet burst into flames, and eventually the entire house burned down.

Kugelmass, unaware of this catastrophe, had his own problems. He had not been thrust into *Portnoy's Complaint,* or into any other novel, for that matter. He had been projected into an old textbook, *Remedial Spanish,* and was running for his life over a barren, rocky terrain as the word *tener* ("to have")—a large and hairy irregular verb—raced after him on its spindly legs.

My Speech
to the Graduates

MORE THAN ANY other time in history, mankind faces a crossroads. One path leads to despair and utter hopelessness. The other, to total extinction. Let us pray we have the wisdom to choose correctly. I speak, by the way, not with any sense of futility, but with a panicky conviction of the absolute meaninglessness of existence which could easily be misinterpreted as pessimism. It is not. It is merely a healthy concern for the predicament of modern man. (Modern man is here defined as any person born after Nietzsche's edict that "God is dead," but before the hit recording "I Wanna Hold Your Hand.") This "predicament" can be stated one of two ways, though certain linguistic philosophers prefer to reduce it to a mathematical equation where it can be easily solved and even carried around in the wallet.

Put in its simplest form, the problem is: How is it possible to find meaning in a finite world given my waist and shirt size? This is a very difficult question when we realize that science has failed us. True, it has conquered many diseases, broken the genetic code, and even placed human beings on the moon, and yet when a man of eighty is left in a room with two eighteen-year-old cocktail waitresses nothing happens. Because the real problems never change. After all, can the human soul be glimpsed through a microscope? Maybe—but you'd definitely need one of those very good ones with two eyepieces. We know that the most advanced computer in the world does not have a brain as sophisticated as that of an ant. True, we could say that of many of our relatives but we only have to put up with them at weddings or special occasions. Science is something we depend on all the time. If I develop a pain in the chest I must take an X-ray. But what if the radiation from the X-ray causes me deeper problems? Before I know it, I'm going in for surgery. Naturally, while they're giving me oxygen an intern decides to light up a cigarette. The next thing you know I'm rocketing over the World Trade Center in bed clothes. Is this science? True, science has taught us how to pasteurize cheese. And true, this can be fun in mixed company—but what of the H-bomb? Have you ever seen what happens when one of those things falls off a desk accidentally? And where is science when one ponders the eternal riddles? How did the cosmos originate? How long has it been around? Did matter begin with an explosion or by the word of God? And if by the latter, could He not have begun it just two weeks earlier to take advantage of some of the warmer weather? Exactly what do we mean when we say, man is mortal? Obviously it's not a compliment.

Religion too has unfortunately let us down. Miguel de Unamuno writes blithely of the "eternal persistence of consciousness," but this is no easy feat. Particularly when reading Thackeray. I often think how comforting life must have been for early man because he believed in a powerful, benevolent Creator who looked after all things. Imagine his disappointment when he saw his wife putting on weight. Contemporary man, of course, has no such peace of mind. He finds himself in the midst of a crisis of faith. He is what we fashionably call "alienated." He has seen the ravages of war, he has known natural catastrophes, he has been to singles bars. My good friend Jacques Monod spoke often of the randomness of the cosmos. He believed everything in existence occurred by pure chance with the possible exception of his breakfast, which he felt certain was made by his housekeeper. Naturally belief in a divine intelligence inspires tranquillity. But this does not free us from our human responsibilities. Am I my brother's keeper? Yes. Interestingly, in my case I share that honor with the Prospect Park Zoo. Feeling godless then, what we have done is made technology God. And yet can technology really be the answer when a brand new Buick, driven by my close associate, Nat Zipsky, winds up in the window of Chicken Delight causing hundreds of customers to scatter? My toaster has never once worked properly in four years. I follow the instructions and push two slices of bread down in the slots and seconds later they rifle upward. Once they broke the nose of a woman I loved very dearly. Are we counting on nuts and bolts and electricity to solve our problems? Yes, the telephone is a good thing—and the refrigerator—and the air conditioner. But not every air conditioner. Not my sister Henny's, for instance. Hers makes a loud noise and still doesn't cool. When the man comes over to fix it, it gets worse. Either that or he tells her she needs a new one. When she complains, he says not to bother him. This man is truly alienated. Not only is he alienated but he can't stop smiling.

The trouble is, our leaders have not adequately prepared us for a mechanized society. Unfortunately our politicians are either incompetent or corrupt. Sometimes both on the same day. The Government is unresponsive to the needs of the little man. Under five-seven, it is impossible to get your Congressman on the phone. I am not denying that democracy is still the finest form of government. In a democracy at least, civil liberties are upheld. No citizen can be wantonly tortured, imprisoned, or made to sit through certain Broadway shows. And yet this is a far cry from what goes on in the Soviet Union. Under their form of totalitarianism, a person merely caught whistling is sentenced to thirty years in a labor camp. If, after fifteen years, he still will not stop whistling, they shoot him. Along with this brutal fascism we find its handmaiden, terrorism. At no other time in history has man been so afraid to cut into his veal chop for fear that it will explode. Violence breeds more violence and it is predicted that by 1990 kidnapping will be the dominant mode of social interaction. Overpopulation will exacerbate problems to the breaking point. Figures tell us there are already more people on earth than we need to move even the heaviest piano. If we do not call a halt to breeding, by the year 2000 there will be no room to serve dinner unless one is willing to set the table on the heads of strangers. Then they must not move for an hour while we eat. Of course energy will be in short supply and each car owner will be allowed only enough gasoline to back up a few inches.

Instead of facing these challenges we turn instead to distractions like drugs and sex. We live in far too permissive a society. Never before has pornography been this rampant. And those films are lit so badly! We are a people who lack defined goals. We have never learned to love. We lack leaders and coherent programs. We have no spiritual center. We are adrift alone in the cosmos wreaking monstrous violence on one another out of frustration and pain. Fortunately, we have not lost our sense of proportion. Summing up, it is clear the future holds great opportunities. It also holds pitfalls. The trick will be to avoid the pitfalls, seize the opportunities, and get back home by six o'clock.

The Diet

ONE DAY, FOR no apparent reason, F. broke his diet. He had gone to lunch at a café with his supervisor, Schnabel, to discuss certain matters. Just what "matters," Schnabel was vague about. Schnabel had called F. the night before, suggesting that they should meet for lunch. "There are various questions," he told him over the phone. "Issues that require resolutions. . . . It can all wait, of course. Perhaps another time." But F. was seized with such a gnawing anxiety over the precise nature and tone of Schnabel's invitation that he insisted they meet immediately.

"Let's have lunch tonight," he said.

"It's nearly midnight," Schnabel told him.

"That's O.K.," F. said. "Of course, we'll have to break into the restaurant."

"Nonsense. It can wait," Schnabel snapped, and hung up.

F. was already breathing heavily. What have

I done, he thought. I've made a fool of myself before Schnabel. By Monday it will be all over the firm. And it's the second time this month I've been made to appear ridiculous.

Three weeks earlier, F. had been discovered in the Xerox room behaving like a woodpecker. Invariably, someone at the office was ridiculing him behind his back. Sometimes, if he turned around rapidly, he would discover thirty or forty coworkers inches away from him with tongues outstretched. Going to work was a nightmare. For one thing, his desk was in the rear, away from the window, and whatever fresh air did reach the dark office was breathed by the other men before F. could inhale it. As he walked down the aisle each day, hostile faces peered at him from behind ledgers and appraised him critically. Once, Traub, a petty clerk, had nodded courteously, and when F. nodded back Traub fired an apple at him. Previously, Traub had obtained the promotion that was promised to F., and had been given a new chair for his desk. F.'s chair, by contrast, had been stolen many years ago, and because of endless bureaucracy he could never seem to requisition another. Since then he stood at his desk each day, hunched over as he typed, realizing the others were making jokes about him. When the incident occurred, F. had asked for a new chair.

"I'm sorry," Schnabel told him, "but you'll have to see the Minister for that."

"Yes, yes, certainly," F. agreed, but when it came time to see the Minister the appointment was postponed. "He can't see you today," an assistant said. "Certain vague notions have arisen and he is not seeing anyone." Weeks went by and F. repeatedly tried to see the Minister, to no avail.

"All I want is a chair," he told his father. "It's not so much that I mind stooping to work, but when I relax and put my feet up on the desk I fall over backward."

"Hogwash," his father said unsympathetically. "If they thought more of you, you'd be seated by now."

"You don't understand!" F. screamed. "I've tried to see the Minister, but he's always busy. And yet when I peep in his window I always see him rehearsing the Charleston."

"The Minister will never see you," his father said, pouring a sherry. "He has no time for weak failures. The truth is, I hear Richter has two chairs. One to sit on at work and one to stroke and hum to."

Richter! F. thought. That fatuous bore, who carried on an illicit love affair for years with the burgomaster's wife, until she found out! Richter had formerly worked at the bank, but certain shortages occurred. At first he had been accused of embezzling. Then it was learned he was eating the money. "It's roughage, isn't it?" he asked the police innocently. He was thrown out of the bank and came to work at F.'s firm, where it was believed that his fluent French made him the ideal man to handle the Parisian accounts. After five years, it became obvious that he couldn't speak a word of French but was merely mouthing non-sense syllables in a fake accent while pursing his lips. Although Richter was demoted, he managed to work his way back into the boss's favor. This time, he convinced his employer that the company could double its profits by merely unlocking the front door and allowing customers to come in.

"Quite a man, this Richter," F.'s father said. "That's why he will always get ahead in the business world, and you will always writhe in frustration like a nauseating, spindly-legged vermin, fit only to be squashed."

F. complimented his father for taking the long view, but later that evening he felt unaccountably depressed. He resolved to diet and make himself look more presentable. Not that he was fat, but subtle insinuations about town had led him to the inescapable notion that in certain circles he might be considered "unpromisingly portly." My father is right, F. thought. I am like some disgusting beetle. No wonder when I asked for a raise Schnabel sprayed me with Raid! I am a wretched, abysmal insect, fit for universal loathing. I deserve to be trampled to death, torn limb from limb by wild animals. I should live under the bed in the dust, or pluck my eyes out in abject shame. Definitely tomorrow I must begin my diet.

That night, F. was the dreamer of euphoric

images. He saw himself thin and able to fit into smart new slacks—the kind that only men with certain reputations could get away with. He dreamed of himself playing tennis gracefully, and dancing with models at fashionable spots. The dream ended with F. strutting slowly across the floor of the Stock Exchange, naked, to the music of Bizet's "Toreador's Song," saying, "Not bad, eh?"

He awoke the next morning in a state of bliss and proceeded to diet for several weeks, reducing his weight by sixteen pounds. Not only did he feel better but his luck seemed to change.

"The Minister will see you," he was told one day.

Ecstatic, F. was brought before the great man and appraised.

"I hear you're into protein," the Minister said.

"Lean meats and, of course, salad," F. responded. "That is to say, an occasional roll—but no butter and certainly no other starches."

"Impressive," the Minister said.

"Not only am I more attractive but I've greatly reduced the chance of heart attack or diabetes," F. said.

"I know all that," the Minister said impatiently.

"Perhaps now I could get certain matters attended to," F. said. "That is, if I maintain my current trim weight."

"We'll see, we'll see," the Minister said. "And

your coffee?" he continued suspiciously. "Do you take it with half-and-half?"

"Oh, no," F. told him. "Skim milk only. I assure you, sir, all my meals are now completely pleasureless experiences."

"Good, good. We'll talk again soon."

That night F. terminated his engagement to Frau Schneider. He wrote her a note explaining that with the sharp drop in his triglyceride level plans they had once made were now impossible. He begged her to understand and said that if his cholesterol count should ever go above one hundred and ninety he would call her.

Then came the lunch with Schnabel—for F., a modest repast consisting of cottage cheese and a peach. When F. asked Schnabel why he had summoned him, the older man was evasive. "Merely to review various alternatives," he said.

"*Which* alternatives?" F. asked. There were no outstanding issues that he could think of, unless he was not remembering them.

"Oh, I don't know. Now it's all becoming hazy and I've quite forgotten the point of the lunch."

"Yes, but I feel you're hiding something," F. said.

"Nonsense. Have some dessert," Schnabel replied.

"No, thank you, Herr Schnabel. That is to say, I'm on a diet."

"How long has it been since you've experienced custard? Or an éclair?"

"Oh, several months," F. said.

"You don't miss them?" Schnabel asked.

"Why, yes. Naturally, I enjoy consummating a meal by ingesting a quantity of sweets. Still, the need for discipline . . . You understand."

"Really?" Schnabel asked, savoring his chocolate-covered pastry, so that F. could feel the man's enjoyment. "It's a pity you're so rigid. Life is short. Wouldn't you like to sample just a bite?" Schnabel was smiling wickedly. He proffered F. a morsel on his fork.

F. felt himself becoming dizzy. "Look here," he said, "I suppose I could always go back on my diet tomorrow."

"Of course, of course," Schnabel said. "That makes splendid sense."

Though F. could have resisted, he succumbed instead. "Waiter," he said, trembling, "an éclair for me, too."

"Good, good," Schnabel said. "That's it! Be one of the boys. Perhaps if you had been more pliable in the past, matters that should have been long resolved would now be finalized—if you know what I mean."

The waiter brought the éclair and placed it before F. F. thought he saw the man wink at Schnabel, but he couldn't be sure. He began eating the gooey dessert, thrilled by every luscious mouthful.

"Nice, isn't it?" Schnabel asked with a knowing smirk. "It's full of calories, of course."

"Yes," F. muttered, wild-eyed and shaking. "It will all go directly to my hips."

"Put it on in your hips, do you?" Schnabel asked.

F. was breathing hard. Suddenly remorse flooded every channel of his body. God in Heaven, what have I done! he thought. I've broken the diet! I've consumed a pastry, knowing full well the implications! Tomorrow I will have to let out my suits!

"Is something wrong, sir?" the waiter asked, smiling along with Schnabel.

"Yes, what is it?" Schnabel asked. "You look as if you've just committed a crime."

"Please, I can't discuss it now! I must have air! Can you get this check, and I'll get the next one."

"Certainly," Schnabel said. "I'll meet you back at the office. I hear the Minister wants to see you about certain charges."

"What? What charges?" F. asked.

"Oh, I don't know exactly. There've been some rumors. Nothing definite. A few questions the authorities need answered. It can wait, of course, if you're still hungry, Tubby."

F. bolted from the table and ran through the streets to his home. He threw himself on the floor before his father and wept. "Father, I have broken my diet!" he cried. "In a moment of weakness, I ordered dessert. Please forgive me! Mercy, I beg of you!"

The Diet

His father listened calmly and said, "I condemn you to death."

"I knew you'd understand," F. said, and with that the two men embraced and reaffirmed their determination to spend more of their free time working with others.

97

The Lunatic's Tale

MADNESS IS A relative state. Who can say which of us is truly insane? And while I roam through Central Park wearing moth-eaten clothes and a surgical mask, screaming revolutionary slogans and laughing hysterically, I wonder even now if what I did was really so irrational. For, dear reader, I was not always what is popularly referred to as "a New York street crazy," pausing at trash cans to fill my shopping bags with bits of string and bottle caps. No, I was once a highly successful doctor living on the upper East Side, gadding about town in a brown Mercedes, and bedecked dashingly in a varied array of Ralph Lauren tweeds. Hard to believe that I, Dr. Ossip Parkis, once a familiar face at theatre openings, Sardi's, Lincoln Center, and the Hamptons, where I boasted great wit and a formidable backhand, am now sometimes seen roller skating unshaven down Broadway wearing a knapsack and a pin-wheel hat.

The dilemma that precipitated this catastrophic fall from grace was simply this. I was living with a woman whom I cared for very deeply and who had a winning and delightful personality and mind; rich in culture and humor and a joy to spend time with. But (and I curse Fate for this) she did not turn me on sexually. Concurrently, I was sneaking crosstown nightly to rendezvous with a photographer's model called Tiffany Schmeederer, whose blood-curdling mentality was in direct inverse proportion to the erotic radiation that oozed from her every pore. Undoubtedly, dear reader, you have heard the expression, "a body that wouldn't quit." Well Tiffany's body would not only not quit, it wouldn't take five minutes off for a coffee break. Skin like satin, or should I say like the finest of Zabar's novy, a leonine mane of chestnut hair, long willowy legs and a shape so curvaceous that to run one's hands over any portion of it was like a ride on the Cyclone. This is not to say the one I roomed with, the scintillating and even profound Olive Chomsky, was a slouch physiognomywise. Not at all. In fact she was a handsome woman with all the attendant perquisites of a charming and witty culture vulture and, crudely put, a mechanic in the sack. Perhaps it was the fact that when the light hit Olive at a certain angle she inexplicably resembled my Aunt Rifka. Not that Olive actually *looked* like my mother's sister. (Rifka had the appearance of a character in Yiddish folklore called the Golem.) It was just that some vague similarity existed around the eyes, and then only if the shadows fell properly. Perhaps it was this incest taboo or perhaps it was just that a face and body like Tiffany Schmeederer's comes along every few million years and usually heralds an ice age or the destruction of the world by fire. The point is, my needs required the best of two women.

It was Olive I met first. And this after an endless string of relationships wherein my partner invariably left something to be desired. My first wife was brilliant, but had no sense of humor. Of the Marx Brothers, she was convinced the amusing one was Zeppo. My second wife was beautiful, but lacked real passion. I recall once, while we were making love, a curious optical illusion occurred and for a split second it almost looked as though she was moving. Sharon Pflug, whom I lived with for three months, was too hostile. Whitney Weisglass was too accommodating. Pippa Mondale, a cheerful divorcée, made the fatal mistake of defending candles shaped like Laurel and Hardy.

Well-meaning friends fixed me up with a relentless spate of blind dates, all unerringly from the pages of H. P. Lovecraft. Ads, answered out of desperation, in the *New York Review of Books*, proved equally futile as the "thirtyish poetess" was sixtyish, the "coed who enjoys Bach and

Beowulf" looked like Grendel, and the "Bay Area bisexual" told me I didn't quite coincide with either of her desires. This is not to imply that now and again an apparent plum would not somehow emerge: a beautiful woman, sensual and wise with impressive credentials and winning ways. But, obeying some age-old law, perhaps from the Old Testament or Egyptian *Book of the Dead, she* would reject *me.* And so it was that I was the most miserable of men. On the surface, apparently blessed with all the necessities for the good life. Underneath, desperately in search of a fulfilling love.

Nights of loneliness led me to ponder the esthetics of perfection. Is anything in nature actually "perfect" with the exception of my Uncle Hyman's stupidity? Who am I to demand perfection? I, with my myriad faults. I made a list of my faults, but could not get past: 1) Sometimes forgets his hat.

Did anyone I know have a "meaningful relationship"? My parents stayed together forty years, but that was out of spite. Greenglass, another doctor at the hospital, married a woman who looked like a Feta cheese "because she's kind." Iris Merman cheated with any man who was registered to vote in the tri-state area. Nobody's relationship could actually be called happy. Soon I began to have nightmares.

I dreamed I visited a singles bar where I was attacked by a gang of roving secretaries. They brandished knives and forced me to say favorable things about the borough of Queens. My analyst counseled compromise. My rabbi said, "Settle, settle. What about a woman like Mrs. Blitzstein? She may not be a great beauty, but nobody is better at smuggling food and light firearms in and out of a ghetto." An actress I met, who assured me her real ambition was to be a waitress at a coffeehouse, seemed promising, but during one brief dinner her single response to everything I said was, "That's zalid." Then one evening, in an effort to unwind after a particularly trying day at the hospital, I attended a Stravinsky concert alone. During intermission I met Olive Chomsky and my life changed.

Olive Chomsky, literate and wry, who quoted Eliot and played tennis and also Bach's "Two Part Inventions" on the piano. And who never said, "Oh, wow," or wore anything marked Pucci or Gucci or listened to country and western music or dialogue radio. And incidentally, who was always willing at the drop of a hat to do the unspeakable and even initiate it. What joyful months spent with her till my sex drive (listed, I believe, in the *Guinness Book of World Records*) waned. Concerts, movies, dinners, weekends, endless wonderful discussions of everything from Pogo to Rig-Veda. And never a gaffe from her lips. Insights only. Wit too! And of course the appropriate hostility toward all deserving targets: politicians, television, facelifts, the architecture of housing projects, men in leisure suits, film courses, and people who begin sentences with "basically."

Oh, curse the day that a wanton ray of light coaxed forth those ineffable facial lines bringing to mind Aunt Rifka's stolid visage. And curse the day also that at a loft party in Soho, an erotic archetype with the unlikely name of Tiffany Schmeederer adjusted the top of her plaid wool kneesock and said to me with a voice resembling that of a mouse in the animated cartoons, "What sign are you?" Hair and fangs audibly rising on my face in the manner of the classic lycanthropic, I felt compelled to oblige her with a brief discussion of astrology, a subject rivaling my intellectual interest with such heavy issues as est, alpha waves, and the ability of leprechauns to locate gold.

Hours later I found myself in a state of waxy flexibility as the last piece of bikini underpants slid noiselessly to the floor around her ankles while I lapsed inexplicably into the Dutch National Anthem. We proceeded to make love in the manner of The Flying Wallendas. And so it began.

Alibis to Olive. Furtive meetings with Tiffany. Excuses for the woman I loved while my lust was spent elsewhere. Spent, in fact, on an empty little yo-yo whose touch and wiggle caused the top of my head to dislodge like a frisbee and hover in space like a flying saucer. I was forsaking my responsibility to the woman of my dreams for a physical obsession not unlike the one Emil Jannings experienced in *The Blue Angel*. Once I feigned illness, asking Olive to attend a Brahms Symphony with her mother so that I could satisfy the moronic whims of my sensual goddess who insisted I drop over to watch "This Is Your Life" on television, "because they're doing Johnny Cash!" Yet, after I paid my dues by sitting through the show, she rewarded me by dimming the rheostats and transporting my libido to the planet Neptune. Another time I casually told Olive I was going out to buy the papers. Then I raced seven blocks to Tiffany's, took the elevator up to her floor, but, as luck would have it, the infernal lift stuck. I paced like a caged cougar between floors, unable to satisfy my flaming desires and also unable to return home by a credible time. Released at last by some firemen, I hysterically concocted a tale for Olive featuring myself, two muggers and the Loch Ness monster.

Fortunately, luck was on my side and she was sleeping when I returned home. Olive's own innate decency made it unthinkable to her that I would deceive her with another woman, and while the frequency of our physical relations had fallen off, I husbanded my stamina in such a manner as to at least partially satisfy her. Constantly ridden with guilt, I offered flimsy alibis about fatigue from overwork, which she bought with the guilelessness of an angel. In truth, the whole ordeal was taking its toll on me as the months went by. I grew to look more and more like the figure in Edvard Munch's "The Scream."

Pity my dilemma, dear reader! This maddening predicament that afflicts perhaps a good many of my contemporaries. Never to find all the requirements one needs in a single member of the opposite sex. On one hand, the yawning abyss of compromise. On the other, the enervating and reprehensible existence of the amorous cheat. Were the French right? Was the trick to have a wife and also a mistress, thereby delegating responsibility for varied needs between two parties? I knew that if I proposed this arrangement openly to Olive, understanding as she was, the chances were very good I would wind up impaled on her British umbrella. I grew weary and depressed and contemplated suicide. I held a pistol to my head, but at the last moment lost my nerve and fired in the air. The bullet passed through my ceiling, causing Mrs. Fitelson in the apartment overhead to leap straight upward onto her bookshelf and remain perched there throughout the high holidays.

Then one night it all cleared up. Suddenly, and with a clarity one usually associates with LSD, my course of action became apparent. I had taken Olive to see a revival of a Bela Lugosi film at the Elgin. In the crucial scene, Lugosi, a mad scientist, switches the brain of some unlucky victim with that of a gorilla, both being strapped to operating tables during an electrical storm. If such a thing could be devised by a screenwriter in the world of fiction, surely a surgeon of my ability could, in real life, accomplish the same thing.

Well, dear reader, I won't bore you with the details which are highly technical and not easily understood by the lay mentality. Suffice it to say that one dark and stormy night a shadowy figure might have been observed smuggling two drugged women (one with a shape that caused men to drive their cars up on the sidewalk) into an unused operating room at Flower Fifth Avenue. There, as bolts of lightning crackled jaggedly through the sky, he performed an operation done before only in the world of celluloid fantasy, and then by a Hungarian actor who would one day turn the hickey into an art form.

The result? Tiffany Schmeederer, her mind now existing in the less spectacular body of Olive Chomsky, found herself delightfully free from the curse of being a sex object. As Darwin taught us, she soon developed a keen intelligence, and while not perhaps the equal of Hannah Arendt's, it did permit her to recognize the follies of astrology and marry happily. Olive Chomsky, suddenly the possessor of a cosmic topography to go with her other superb gifts, became my wife as I became the envy of all around me.

The only hitch was that after several months of bliss with Olive that was the equal of anything in the *Arabian Nights,* I inexplicably grew dissatisfied with this dream woman and developed instead a crush on Billie Jean Zapruder, an airline stewardess whose boyish, flat figure and Alabama twang caused my heart to do flip-flops. It was at this point that I resigned my position at the hospital, donned my pinwheel hat and knapsack and began skating down Broadway.

Reminiscences:
Places and People

BROOKLYN: TREE-LINED STREETS. The Bridge. Churches and cemeteries everywhere. And candy stores. A small boy helps a bearded old man across the street and says, "Good Sabbath." The old man smiles and empties his pipe on the boy's head. The child runs crying into his house. . . . Stifling heat and humidity descend on the borough. Residents bring folding chairs out onto the street after dinner to sit and talk. Suddenly it begins to snow. Confusion sets in. A vender wends his way down the street selling hot pretzels. He is set upon by dogs and chased up a tree. Unfortunately for him, there are more dogs at the top of the tree.

"Benny! Benny!" A mother is calling her son. Benny is sixteen but already has a police record. When he is twenty-six, he will go to the electric chair. At thirty-six, he will be hanged. At fifty, he will own his own dry-cleaning store. Now his mother serves breakfast, and because the family is too poor to afford fresh rolls he spreads marmalade on the *News*.

Ebbets Field: Fans line Bedford Avenue in hopes of retrieving home-run balls hit over the right-field wall. After eight scoreless innings, there is a roar from the crowd. A ball sails over the wall, and eager fans jostle for it! For some reason, it is a football—no one knows why. Later that season, the owner of the Brooklyn Dodgers will trade his shortstop to Pittsburgh for a left fielder, and then he will trade himself to Boston for the owner of the Braves and his two youngest children.

Sheepshead Bay: A leathery-faced man laughs heartily and hauls up his crab traps. A giant crab seizes the man's nose between his claws. The man is no longer laughing. His friends pull him from one side while the crab's friends pull from the other. It is no use. The sun sets. They are still at it.

New Orleans: A jazz band stands in the rain at a cemetery playing mournful hymns as a body is lowered into the earth. Now they strike up a spirited march and begin the parade back to town. Halfway there, someone realizes they have buried the wrong man. What's more, they weren't even close. The person they buried was not dead, or even sick; in fact, he was yodelling at the time. They return to the cemetery and exhume the poor man, who threatens to sue, although they promise to let him have his suit cleaned and send them the bill. Meanwhile, no one knows which person is actually dead. The band continues to play while each of the onlookers is buried in turn, on the theory that the deceased will go down the smoothest. Soon it becomes apparent that no one has died, and now it is too late to get a body, because of the holiday rush.

It is Mardi Gras. Creole food everywhere. Crowds in costume jam the streets. A man dressed as a shrimp is thrown into a steaming pot of bisque. He protests, but no one believes he is not a crustacean. Finally he produces a driver's license and is released.

Beauregard Square is teeming with sightseers. Once Marie Laveau practiced voodoo here. Now an old Haitian "conjure man" is selling dolls and amulets. A policeman tells him to move on, and an argument begins. When it is over, the policeman is four inches tall. Outraged, he still tries to make an arrest, but his voice is so high that no one can understand him. Presently a cat crosses the street, and the policeman is forced to run for his life.

Paris: Wet pavements. And lights—everywhere there are lights! I come upon a man at an outdoor café. It is André Malraux. Oddly, he thinks that I am André Malraux. I explain that he is Malraux and I am just a student. He is relieved to hear this, as he is fond of Mme. Malraux and would hate to think she is my wife. We talk of serious things, and he tells me that man is free to choose his own fate and that not until he realizes that death is part of life can he really understand existence. Then he offers to sell me a rabbit's foot. Years later, we meet at a dinner, and again he insists that I am Malraux. This time, I go along with it and get to eat his fruit cocktail.

Autumn. Paris is crippled by another strike. Now it is the acrobats. No one is tumbling, and the city comes to a standstill. Soon the strike spreads to include jugglers, and then ventriloquists. Parisians regard these as essential services, and many students become violent. Two Algerians are caught practicing handstands and their heads are shaved.

A ten-year-old girl with long brown curls and green eyes hides a plastic explosive device in the Minister of the Interior's chocolate mousse. With the first bite, he passes through the roof of Fouquet's and lands unharmed in Les Halles. Now Les Halles is no more.

Through Mexico by auto: The poverty is staggering. Clusters of sombreros evoke the murals of Orozco. It is over a hundred degrees in the shade. A poor Indian sells me a fried-pork enchilada. It tastes delicious, and I wash it down with some ice water. I feel a slight queasiness in the stomach and then start speaking Dutch. Suddenly a mild abdominal pain causes me to snap over like a book slamming shut. Six months later, I awake in a Mexican hospital completely bald and clutching a Yale pennant. It has been a fearful experience, and I am told that when I was delirious with fever and close to death's door I ordered two suits from Hong Kong.

I recuperate in a ward full of many wonderful peasants, several of whom will later become close friends. There is Alfonso, whose mother wanted him to be a matador. He was gored by a bull and then later gored by his mother. And Juan, a simple pig farmer who could not write his name but somehow managed to defraud I.T.T. out of six million dollars. And old Hernández, who had ridden beside Zapata for many years, until the great revolutionary had him arrested for constantly kicking him.

Rain. Six straight days of rain. Then fog. I sit in a London pub with Willie Maugham. I am distressed, because my first novel, *Proud Emetic,* has been coolly received by the critics. Its one favorable notice, in the *Times,* was vitiated by the last sentence, which called the book "a miasma of asinine clichés unrivalled in Western letters."

Maugham explains that while this quote can be interpreted many ways, it might be best not to use it in the print ads. Now we stroll up Old Brompton Road, and the rains come again. I offer my umbrella to Maugham and he takes it, despite the fact he already has an umbrella. Maugham now carries two open umbrellas while I run along beside him.

"One must never take criticism too seriously,"

he tells me. "My first short story was harshly denounced by one particular critic. I brooded and made caustic remarks about the man. Then one day I reread the story and realized he had been correct. It *was* shallow and badly constructed. I never forgot the incident, and years later, when the Luftwaffe was bombing London, I shone a light on the critic's house."

Maugham pauses to buy and open a third umbrella. "In order to be a writer," he continues, "one must take chances and not be afraid to look foolish. I wrote *The Razor's Edge* while wearing a paper hat. In the first draft of *Rain,* Sadie Thompson was a parrot. We grope. We take risks. All I had when I began *Of Human Bondage* was the conjunction 'and.' I knew a story with 'and' in it could be delightful. Gradually the rest took shape."

A gust of wind lifts Maugham off his feet and slams him into a building. He chuckles. Maugham then offers the greatest advice anyone could give to a young author: "At the end of an interrogatory sentence, place a question mark. You'd be surprised how effective it can be."

Nefarious Times We Live In

YES. I CONFESS. It was I, Willard Pogrebin, mild mannered and promising at one time in life, who fired a shot at the President of the United States. Fortunately for all concerned, a member of the onlooking crowd jostled the Luger in my hand causing the bullet to ricochet off a McDonald's sign and lodge in some bratwurst at Himmelstein's Sausage Emporium. After a light scuffle in which several G-men laced my trachea into a reef knot, I was subdued and carted off for observation.

How did it happen that I had come to this, you ask? Me, a character with no pronounced political convictions; whose childhood ambition was to play Mendelssohn on the cello or perhaps dance on point in the great capitals of the world? Well, it all began two years ago. I had just been medically discharged from the army, the results of certain scientific experiments performed on me without my knowledge. More precisely, a group of us had been fed roast chicken stuffed with lysergic acid, in a research program designed to determine the quantity of LSD a man can ingest before he attempts to fly over the World Trade Center. Developing secret weapons is of great importance to the Pentagon and the previous week I had been shot with a dart whose drugged tip caused me to look and talk exactly like Salvador Dali. Cumulative side effects took their toll on my perception and when I could no longer tell the difference between my brother Morris and two soft-boiled eggs, I was discharged.

Electroshock therapy at the Veterans Hospital helped although wires got crossed with a behavioral psychology lab and I along with several chimpanzees all performed *The Cherry Orchard* together in perfect English. Broke and alone upon my release, I recall hitchhiking west and being picked up by two native Californians: a charismatic young man with a beard like Rasputin's and a charismatic young woman with a beard like Svengali's. I was exactly what they were looking for, they explained, as they were in the process of transcribing the Kaballah on parchment and had run out of blood. I tried to explain that I was en route to Hollywood seeking honest employment but the combination of their hypnotic eyes and a knife the size of a sculling oar convinced me of their sincerity. I recall being driven to a deserted ranch where several mesmerized young women force fed me organic health foods and then tried to emboss the sign of the penta-gram on my forehead with a soldering iron. I then witnessed a black mass in which hooded adoles-cent acolytes chanted the words, "Oh wow," in Latin. I also recall being made to take peyote and cocaine and eat a white substance that came from boiled cactus, which caused my head to revolve completely around like a radar dish. Further de-tails escape me, although my mind was clearly affected as two months later I was arrested in Beverly Hills for trying to marry an oyster.

Upon my release from police custody I longed for some inner peace in an attempt to preserve what remained of my precarious sanity. More than once I had been solicited by ardent prosely-tizers on the street to seek religious salvation with the Reverend Chow Bok Ding, a moon-faced charismatic, who combined the teachings of Lao-Tze with the wisdom of Robert Vesco. An esthetic man who renounced all worldly possessions in excess of those owned by Charles Foster Kane, the Reverend Ding explained his two modest goals. One was to instill in all his followers the values of prayer, fasting, and brotherhood and the other was to lead them in a religious war against the NATO countries. After attending several ser-mons, I noticed that Reverend Ding thrived on robotlike fealty and any diminution of divine fervor met with raised eyebrows. When I men-tioned that it seemed to me the Reverend's fol-lowers were being systematically turned into mind-less zombies by a fraudulent megalomaniac, it was taken as criticism. Moments later I was led swiftly by my lower lip into a devotional shrine, where certain minions of the Reverend who resembled Sumo wrestlers suggested I rethink my position for a few weeks with no petty distractions like food or water. To further underscore the general sense of disappointment with my attitude, a fist full of quarters was applied to my gums with pneumatic regularity. Ironically, the only thing that kept me from going insane was the constant repeating of my private mantra, which was "Yoicks." Finally, I succumbed to the terror and began to hallucinate. I recall seeing Frankenstein stroll through Covent Gardens with a hamburger on skis.

Four weeks later I awoke in a hospital reasonably O.K. except for a few bruises and the firm conviction that I was Igor Stravinsky. I learned the Reverend Ding had been sued by a fifteen-year-old Maharishi over the question of which of them was actually God and therefore entitled to free passes to Loew's Orpheum. The issue was finally resolved with the help of the Bunco Squad and both gurus were apprehended as they tried to beat it across the border to Nirvana, Mexico.

By this time, although physically intact, I had developed the emotional stability of Caligula and hoping to rebuild my shattered psyche, I volunteered for a program called PET—Perlemutter's Ego Therapy, named after its charismatic founder, Gustave Perlemutter. Perlemutter had been a former bop saxophonist and had come to psychotherapy late in life but his method had attracted many famous film stars who swore that it changed them much more rapidly and in a deeper way than even the astrology column in *Cosmopolitan*.

A group of neurotics, most of whom had struck out with more conventional treatment, were driven to a pleasant rural spa. I suppose I should have suspected something from the barbed wire and the Dobermans but Perlemutter's underlings assured us that the screaming we heard was purely primal. Forced to sit upright in hard-backed chairs with no relief for seventy-two straight hours, our resistance gradually crumpled and it was not long before Perlemutter was reading us passages from *Mein Kampf*. As time passed it was clear that he was a total psychotic whose therapy consisted of sporadic admonitions to "cheer up."

Several of the more disillusioned ones tried to leave but to their chagrin found the surrounding fences electrified. Although Perlemutter insisted he was a doctor of the mind, I noticed he kept receiving phone calls from Yassir Arafat and were it not for a last minute raid on the premises by agents of Simon Wiesenthal there is no telling what might have happened.

Tense and understandably cynical by the turn of events, I took up residence in San Francisco, earning money in the only way I now could, by agitating at Berkeley and informing for the FBI. For several months I sold and resold bits of information to federal agents, mostly concerning a CIA plan to test the resiliency of New York City residents by dropping potassium cyanide in the reservoir. Between this and an offer to be dialogue coach on a snuff porn movie, I could just make ends meet. Then one evening, as I opened my door to put out the garbage, two men leaped stealthily from the shadows and draping a furniture pad over my head, hustled me off in the trunk of a car. I remember being jabbed with a needle and before I blacked out hearing voices comment that I seemed heavier than Patty but lighter than Hoffa. I awakened to find myself in a dark closet where I was forced to undergo total sensory deprivation for three weeks. Following that I was tickled by experts and two men sang country and western music to me until I agreed to do anything they wanted. I cannot vouch for what ensued as it is possible it was all a result of my brainwashing but I was then brought into a room where President Gerald Ford shook my hand and asked me if I would follow him around the country and take a shot at him now and then, being careful to miss. He said it would give him a chance to act bravely and could serve as a distraction from genuine issues, which he felt unequipped to deal with. In my weakened condition I agreed to anything. Two days later the incident at Himmelstein's Sausage Emporium occurred.

A Giant Step
for Mankind

LUNCHING YESTERDAY ON chicken in ichor—a house specialty at my favorite midtown restaurant—I was forced to listen to a playwright acquaintance defend his latest opus against a set of notices that read like a Tibetan *Book of the Dead*. Drawing tenuous connections between Sophocles' dialogue and his own, Moses Goldworm wolfed down his vegetable cutlet and raged like Carrie Nation against the New York theatre critics. I, of course, could do nothing more than offer a sympathetic ear and assure him that the phrase "a dramatist of zero promise" might be interpreted in several ways. Then, in the split second it takes to go from calm to bedlam, the Pinero manqué half rose from his seat, suddenly unable to speak. Frantically waving his arms and clutching his throat, the poor fellow turned a shade of blue invariably associated with Thomas Gainsborough.

"My God, what is it?" someone screamed, as silverware clattered to the floor and heads turned from every table.

"He's having a coronary!" a waiter yelled.

"No, no, it's a fit," said a man at the booth next to me.

Goldworm continued to struggle and wave his arms, but with ever-diminishing style. Then, as various mutually exclusive remedies were advanced in anxious falsettos by sundry well-meaning hysterics in the room, the playwright confirmed the waiter's diagnosis by collapsing to the floor like a sack of rivets. Crumpled in a forlorn heap, Goldworm seemed destined to slip away before an ambulance could arrive, when a six-foot stranger possessing the cool aplomb of an astronaut strode to stage center and said in dramatic tones, "Leave everything to me, folks. We don't need a doctor—this is not a cardiac problem. By clutching his throat, this fellow has made the universal sign, known in every corner of the world, to indicate that he is choking. The symptoms may appear to be the same as those of a man suffering from a heart attack, but this man, I assure you, can be saved by the Heimlich Maneuver!"

With that, the hero of the moment wrapped his arms around my companion from behind and lifted him to an upright position. Placing his fist just under Goldworm's sternum, he hugged sharply, causing a side order of bean curd to rocket out of the victim's trachea and carom off the hat rack. Goldworm came to apace and thanked his savior, who then directed our attention to a printed notice, supplied by the Board of Health, affixed to the wall. The poster described the aforementioned drama with perfect fidelity. What we had witnessed was indeed "the universal choking signal," conveying the victim's tripartite plight: (1) Cannot speak or breathe, (2) Turns blue, (3) Collapses. The diagnostic signs on the notice were followed by clear directions on the administration of the lifesaving procedure: the selfsame abrupt hug and resulting airborne protein we had witnessed, which had relieved Goldworm of the awkward formalities of the Long Goodbye.

A few minutes later, strolling home on Fifth Avenue, I wondered if Dr. Heimlich, whose name is now so firmly placed in the national consciousness as the discoverer of the marvellous maneuver I had just seen performed, had any idea of how close he had once come to being scooped by three still utterly anonymous scientists who had worked for months on end in search of a cure for the same perilous mealtime trauma. I also wondered if he knew of the existence of a certain diary kept by an unnamed member of the pioneer trio—a diary that came into my possession at auction quite by mistake, because of its similarity in heft and color to an illustrated work entitled "Harem Slaves," for which I had bid a trifling eight weeks' salary. Following are some excerpts from the diary, which I set down here purely in the interest of science:

JANUARY 3. Met my two colleagues today for the first time and found them both enchanting, although Wolfsheim is not at all as I had imagined. For one thing, he is heavier than in his photo (I think he uses an old one). His beard is of a medium length but seems to grow with the irrational abandon of crabgrass. Add to this thick, bushy brows and beady eyes the size of microbes, which dart about suspiciously behind spectacles the thickness of bulletproof glass. And then there are the twitches. The man has accumulated a repertoire of facial tics and blinks that demand nothing less than a complete musical score by Stravinsky. And yet Abel Wolfsheim is a brilliant scientist whose work on dinner-table choking has made him a legend the world over. He was quite flattered that I was familiar with his paper on Random Gagging, and he confided to me that my once skeptically regarded theory, that hiccupping is innate, is now commonly accepted at M.I.T.

If Wolfsheim is eccentric-looking, however, the other member of our triumvirate is exactly what I had expected from reading her work. Shulamith Arnolfini, whose experiments with recombinant DNA led to the creation of a gerbil that could sing "Let My People Go," is British in the extreme—predictably tweedy, with her hair skun in a bun, and with horn-rimmed glasses resting halfway down a beak nose. Furthermore, she possesses a speech impediment so audibly juicy that to be near her when she pronounces a word like "sequestered" is equivalent to standing at the center of a monsoon. I like them both and I predict great discoveries.

JANUARY 5. Things did not get under way as smoothly as I had hoped, for Wolfsheim and I have had a mild disagreement over procedure. I suggested doing our initial experiments on mice, but he regards this as unnecessarily timid. His idea is to use convicts, feeding them large chunks of meat at five-second intervals, with instructions not to chew before swallowing. Only then, he claims, can we observe the dimensions of the problem in its true perspective. I took issue on moral grounds, and Wolfsheim became defensive. I asked him if he felt science was above morality, and took issue with his equating humans and hamsters. Nor did I agree with his somewhat emotional assessment of me as a "unique moron." Fortunately, Shulamith took my side.

JANUARY 7. Today was a productive one for Shulamith and me. Working around the clock, we induced strangulation in a mouse. This was accomplished by coaxing the rodent to ingest healthy portions of Gouda cheese and then making it laugh. Predictably, the food went down the wrong pipe, and choking occurred. Grasping the mouse firmly by the tail, I snapped it like a small whip, and the morsel of cheese came loose. Shulamith and I made voluminous notes on the experiment. If we can transfer the tailsnap procedure to humans, we may have something. Too early to tell.

FEBRUARY 15. Wolfsheim has developed a theory that he insists on testing, although I find it simplistic. He is convinced that a person choking on food can be saved by (his words) "giving the victim a drink of water." At first I thought he was joking, but his intense manner and wild eyes indicated a definite commitment to the concept. Clearly, he has been up for days toying with this notion, and in his laboratory glasses of water filled to various levels were everywhere. When I responded skeptically, he accused me of being negative, and began twitching like a disco dancer. You can tell he hates me.

FEBRUARY 27. Today was a day off, and Shulamith and I decided to motor to the countryside. Once we were out in nature, the whole concept of choking seemed so far away. Shulamith told me that she had been married before, to a scientist who had pioneered a study of radioactive isotopes, and whose entire body vanished in mid-conversation while he was testifying before a Senate committee. We talked about our personal preferences and tastes and discovered that we were both fond of the same bacteria. I asked Shulamith how she would feel if I kissed her. She said, "Swell," giving me the full moist spray peculiar to her speech problem. I have come to the conclusion that she is quite a beautiful woman, particularly when viewed through an X-ray-proof lead screen.

MARCH 1. I now believe Wolfsheim is a madman. He tested his "glass of water" theory a dozen times, and in no case did it prove effective. When I told him to stop wasting valuable time and money, he bounced a petri dish off the bridge of my nose, and I was forced to hold him at bay with the Bunsen burner. As always, when work becomes more difficult frustrations mount.

MARCH 3. Unable to obtain subjects for our dangerous experiments, we have been forced to cruise restaurants and cafeterias, hoping to work rapidly should we be lucky enough to find someone in distress. At the Sans Souci Deli, I tried lifting a Mrs. Rose Moscowitz by her ankles and shaking her, and although I managed to dislodge a monstrous chunk of kasha, she seemed ungrateful. Wolfsheim suggested that we might try slapping choke victims on the back, and pointed out that important back-slapping concepts had been suggested to him by Fermi at a symposium on digestion in Zurich thirty-two years ago. A grant to explore this was refused, however, when the government decided in favor of nuclear priorities. Wolfsheim, incidentally, has turned out to be a rival in my affair with Shulamith, and confessed affection for her yesterday in the biology lab. When he tried to kiss her, she hit him with a frozen monkey. He is a very complex and sad man.

MARCH 18. At Marcello's Villa today we chanced upon a Mrs. Guido Bertoni in the act of choking on what was later identified as either cannelloni or a Ping-Pong ball. As I had foreseen, slapping her on the back did not help. Wolfsheim, unable to part with the old theories, tried administering a glass of water, but unfortunately seized it from the table of a gentleman well placed in the cement and contracting community, and all three of us were escorted out of the service entrance and up against a lamppost, over and over.

APRIL 2. Today Shulamith raised the notion of a pincers—that is, some form of long tweezers or forceps to extract food that falls into the windpipe. Each citizen would carry one such instrument on his person and be educated in its use and handling by the Red Cross. In eager anticipation, we drove to Belknap's Salt of the Sea to remove a badly wedged crabcake from the esophagus of a Mrs. Faith Blitzstein. Unfortunately, the gasping woman became agitated when I produced the formidable tweezers, and sank her teeth into my wrist, causing me to drop the instrument down her throat. Only the quick action of her husband, Nathan, who held her above the ground by her hair and raised and lowered her like a yo-yo, prevented a fatality.

APRIL 11. Our project is coming to a close— unsuccessfully, I am sorry to say. Funding has been cut off, our foundation board having decided that the remaining money might be more profitably spent on some joy-buzzers. After I received the news of our termination, I had to have fresh air to clear my head, and as I walked alone at night by the Charles River I couldn't help reflecting on the limits of science. Perhaps people are *meant* to choke now and then when they eat. Perhaps it is all part of some unfathomable cosmic design. Are we so conceited as to think research and science can control everything? A man swallows too large a bite of steak, and gags. What could be simpler? What more proof is needed of the exquisite harmony of the universe? We will never know all the answers.

APRIL 20. Yesterday afternoon was our last day, and I chanced upon Shulamith in the Commissary, where she was glancing over a monograph on the new herpes vaccine and gobbling a matjes herring to tide her over till dinnertime. I approached stealthily from the rear and, seeking to surprise her, quietly placed my arms around her, experiencing at that moment the bliss that only a lover feels. Instantly she began choking, a portion of herring having lodged suddenly in her gullet. My arms were still around her, and, as fate would have it, my hands were clasped just under her sternum. Something—call it blind instinct, call it scientific luck—made me form a fist and snap it back against her chest. In a trice, the herring became disengaged, and a moment later the lovely woman was as good as new. When I told Wolfsheim about this, he said, "Yes, of course. It works with herring, but will it work with ferrous metals?"

I don't know what he meant and I don't care. The project is ended, and while it is perhaps true that we have failed, others will follow in our footsteps and, building upon our crude preliminary work, will at last succeed. Indeed, all of us here can foresee the day when our children, or certainly our grandchildren, will live in a world where no individual, regardless of race, creed, or color, will ever be fatally overcome by his own main course. To end on a personal note, Shulamith and I are going to marry, and until the economy begins to brighten a little she and Wolfsheim and I have decided to provide a much-needed service and open up a really first-class tattoo parlor.

The Shallowest Man

SITTING AROUND THE delicatessen, discussing shallow people we had known, Koppelman brought up the name of Lenny Mendel. Koppelman said Mendel was positively the shallowest human he'd ever come across, bar none, and then proceeded to relate the following story.

For years there was a weekly poker game amongst roughly the same personnel. It was a small stakes game played for fun and relaxation at a rented hotel room. The men bet and bluffed, ate and drank, and talked of sex and sports and business. After a while (and no one could pinpoint the exact week) the players began to notice that one of them, Meyer Iskowitz, was not looking too well. When they commented on it, Iskowitz pooh-poohed the whole thing.

"I'm fine, I'm fine," he said. "Whose bet?"

But as a few months passed he grew progressively worse looking and when he didn't show up to play one week the message was that he had checked into the hospital with hepatitis. Everyone sensed the ominous truth and so it was not a complete surprise three weeks later when Sol Katz phoned Lenny Mendel at the TV show where he worked and said, "Poor Meyer has cancer. The lymph nodes. A bad kind. It's already spread over his body. He's up at Sloan-Kettering."

"How horrible," Mendel said, shaken and suddenly depressed as he sipped weakly from his malted on the other end of the phone.

"Sol and I went to see him today. Poor guy has no family. And he looks awful. He was always robust too. Oy, what a world. Anyhow, it's Sloan-Kettering. 1275 York and visiting hours are twelve to eight."

Katz hung up, leaving Lenny Mendel in a gloomy mood. Mendel was forty-four and healthy as far as he knew. (Suddenly he was qualifying his self-assessment so as not to jinx himself.) He was only six years younger than Iskowitz and though the two were not terribly close they had shared many laughs over cards once a week for five years. The poor man, Mendel thought. I guess I should send some flowers. He instructed Dorothy, one of the secretaries at NBC, to call the florist and handle the details. The news of Iskowitz's imminent death weighed heavily over Mendel that afternoon, but what was beginning to gnaw at him and unnerve him even more was the unshakable realization that he would be expected to visit his poker crony.

What an unpleasant chore, Mendel thought. He felt guilty over his desire to avoid the whole business and yet he dreaded seeing Iskowitz under these circumstances. Of course Mendel understood that all men die and even took some comfort from a paragraph he had once come across in a book that said death is not in opposition to life but a natural part of it; yet when he actually focused on the fact of his own eternal annihilation it caused him to feel limitless panic. He was not religious and not a hero and not a stoic, and during the course of his day-to-day existence he didn't want to know from funerals or hospitals or terminal wards. If a hearse went by in the street the image might stay with him for hours. Now he pictured Meyer Iskowitz's wasted figure in front of him and himself awkwardly trying to make jokes or conversation. How he hated hospitals with their functional tile and institutional lighting. All that hush-hush, quiet atmosphere. And always too warm. Suffocating. And the lunch trays and the bedpans and the elderly and lame shuffling in white gowns through the halls, the heavy air saturated with exotic germs. And what if all the speculation of cancer being a virus is true? I should be in the same room as Meyer Iskowitz? Who knows if it's catching? Let's face it. What the hell do they know about this awful disease? Nothing. So one day they'll find that one of its admittedly myriad forms is transmitted by Iskowitz coughing on me. Or clasping my hand to his chest. The thought of Iskowitz expiring be-

fore his eyes horrified him. He saw his once
hearty, now emaciated acquaintance (suddenly he
was an acquaintance, not actually a friend) gasping a last breath and reaching out to Mendel saying, "Don't let me go—don't let me go!" Jesus,
Mendel thought as his forehead beaded up with
sweat. I don't relish visiting Meyer. And why the
hell must I? We were never close. For God's
sake, I saw the man once a week. Strictly for
cards. We rarely exchanged more than a few
words. He was a poker hand. In five years we
never saw one another outside the hotel room.
Now he's dying, and suddenly it's incumbent
upon me to pay a visit. All of a sudden we're
buddies. Intimate yet. I mean, for God's sake, he
was tighter with every other person in that game.
If anything, I was *least* close to him. Let them
visit him. After all, how much traffic does a
sick man need? Hell, he's dying. He wants quiet,
not a parade of empty well-wishers. Anyhow I
can't go today because there's a dress rehearsal.
What do they think I am, a man of leisure? I've
just been made associate producer. I got a million
things on my mind. And the next few days are
out too because it's the Christmas show and it's
a madhouse here. So I'll do it next week. What's
the big deal? The end of next week. Who knows?
Will he even live till the end of next week? Well
if he does I'll be there and if not, what the hell's
the difference? If that's a hard line, well, then
life's hard. Meanwhile the opening monologue on
the show needs punching up. Topical humor. The

show needs more topical humor. Not so many brand-name jokes.

Using one rationale or another, Lenny Mendel avoided visiting Meyer Iskowitz for two-and-a-half weeks. When his obligation rose more strongly to mind he felt very guilty and worse even yet when he caught himself half hoping that he would receive the news that it was over and Iskowitz had died, thereby getting him off the hook. It's a sure thing anyhow, he reasoned, so why not right away? Why should the man linger and suffer? I mean I know it sounds heartless, he thought to himself, and I know I'm weak, but some people can handle these things better than others. Visits to the dying that is. It's depressing. And like I don't have enough on my mind.

But the news of Meyer's death did not come. Only guilt-provoking remarks by his friends at the poker game.

"Oh, you haven't seen him yet? You really ought to. He gets so few visitors and he's so appreciative."

"He always looked up to you, Lenny."

"Yeah, he always liked Lenny."

"I know you must be very busy with the show but you should try and get up to see Meyer. After all, how much time does the man have left?"

"I'll go tomorrow," Mendel said, but when it came time he pushed it off again. The truth is, when he finally got up enough courage to make a ten-minute visit to the hospital it was more out of needing to have a self-image that he could live

with rather than out of any compassion for Iskowitz. Mendel knew that if Iskowitz died and he
had been too scared or disgusted to visit him, he
might regret his cowardice and it would then all
be irrevocable. I will hate myself for being spine-
less, he thought, and the others will know me for
what I am—a self-centered louse. On the other
hand, if I visit Iskowitz and act like a man, I will
be a better person in my own eyes and in the eyes
of the world. The point is that Iskowitz's need for
comfort and companionship was not the force
behind the visit.

Now the story takes a turn because we're discussing shallowness, and the dimensions of Lenny
Mendel's record-breaking superficiality are just
beginning to emerge. On a cold Tuesday evening
at seven-fifty (so he couldn't visit more than ten
minutes even if he wanted to) Mendel received
from hospital security the laminated pass that
allowed him access to room 1501 where Meyer
Iskowitz lay alone in bed, surprisingly decent
looking considering the stage to which his illness
had advanced.

"How's it going, Meyer?" Mendel said weakly
as he tried to maintain a respectable distance
from the bed.

"Who's that? Mendel? Is that you, Lenny?"

"I been busy. Otherwise I'd have come sooner."

"Oh it's so nice of you to bother. I'm so glad
to see you."

"How are you, Meyer?"

"How am I? I'm going to beat this thing,

Lenny. Mark my words. I'm going to beat this thing."

"Sure you will, Meyer," Lenny Mendel said in a feeble voice, constricted by tension. "In six months you'll be back cheating at cards. Ha, ha, no seriously, you never cheated." Keep it light, Mendel thought, keep the one-liners coming. Treat him like he isn't dying, Mendel thought, recalling advice he had read on the subject. In the stuffy little room, Mendel imagined he was inhaling billows of the virulent cancer germs as they emanated from Iskowitz and multiplied in the warm air. "I bought you a *Post*," Lenny said, laying the offering down on the table.

"Sit, sit. Where you running? You just came," Meyer said warmly.

"I'm not running. It's just that the visiting instructions say to keep the visits short for the comfort of the patients."

"So what's new?" Meyer asked.

Resigned to chat the full time till eight, Mendel pulled up a chair (not too close) and tried to make conversation about cards, sports, headlines, and finances, always awkwardly conscious of the overriding, horrible fact that, despite Iskowitz's optimism, he would never be leaving this hospital alive. Mendel was perspiring and felt woozy. The pressure, the forced gaiety, the pervasive sense of disease and awareness of his own fragile mortality caused his neck to grow stiff and his mouth to dry up. He wanted to leave. It was already five after eight and he hadn't been asked to go. The visiting rules were lax. He squirmed in his seat as Iskowitz spoke softly of the old days and after five more depressing minutes Mendel thought he would faint. Then, just when it seemed he could stand it no longer, a momentous event occurred. The nurse, Miss Hill—the twenty-four-year-old, blond, blue-eyed nurse with her long hair and magnificently beautiful face—walked in and, fixing Lenny Mendel with a warm, ingratiating smile, said, "Visiting hours are over. You'll have to say goodbye." Right then Lenny Mendel, who had never seen a more exquisite creature in all his life, fell in love. It was as simple as that. He gaped, open-mouthed, with the stunned appearance of a man who had finally set eyes on the woman of his dreams. Mendel's heart virtually ached with an overwhelming feeling of the most profound longing. My God, he thought, it's like in a movie. And there was no question about it either, Miss Hill was absolutely adorable. Sexy and curvaceous in her white uniform, she had big eyes and lush, sensual lips. She had good, high cheekbones and perfectly shaped breasts. Her voice was sweet and charming as she straightened up the sheets, teasing Meyer Iskowitz good-naturedly while she projected warm concern for the sick man. Finally she picked up the food tray and left, pausing only to wink at Lenny Mendel and whisper, "Better go. He needs rest."

"This is your usual nurse?" Mendel asked Iskowitz after she was gone.

"Miss Hill? She's new. Very cheerful. I like

her. Not sour like some of the others here. Friendly as they come. And a good sense of humor. Well, you better go. It was such a pleasure seeing you, Lenny."

"Yeah, right. You too, Meyer."

Mendel rose in a daze and walked down the corridor hoping to run into Miss Hill before he reached the elevators. She was nowhere to be found and when Mendel hit the street with its cool night air he knew he would have to see her again. My God, he thought, as he cabbed home through Central Park, I know actresses, I know models, and here a young nurse is more lovely than all the others put together. Why didn't I speak to her? I should have engaged her in conversation. I wonder if she's married? Well no—not if it's *Miss* Hill. I should've asked Meyer about her. Of course, if she's new . . . He ran through all the "should-haves" imagining he blew some kind of big chance but then consoled himself with the fact that at least he knew where she worked and he could locate her again when he regained his poise. It occurred to him that she might finally prove unintelligent or dull like so many of the beautiful women he met in show business. Of course she is a nurse which could mean her concerns are deeper, more humane, less egotistical. Or it could mean that if I knew her better she'd be an unimaginative purveyor of bedpans. No—life can't be that cruel. He toyed with the notion of waiting for her outside the hospital but guessed that her shifts would change and that he'd miss her. Also that he might put her off if he accosted her.

He returned the following day to visit Isko-witz, bringing him a book called *Great Sport Stories,* which he felt made his visit less suspicious. Iskowitz was surprised and delighted to see him but Miss Hill was not on that night and instead a virago named Miss Caramanulis floated in and out of the room. Mendel could hardly conceal his disappointment and tried to remain interested in what Iskowitz had to say but couldn't. Iskowitz being a bit sedated never noticed Mendel's dis-tracted anxiousness to leave.

Mendel returned the next day and found the heavenly subject of his fantasies in attendance with Iskowitz. He made some stammering con-versation and when he was about to leave did manage to get next to her in the corridor. Eaves-dropping on her conversation with another young nurse, Mendel seemed to get the impression that she had a boyfriend and the two were going to see a musical the following day. Trying to appear casual as he waited for the elevator, Mendel listened carefully to find out how serious the rela-tionship was but could never hear all the details. He did seem to think she was engaged and while she had no ring he thought he heard her refer to someone as "my fiancé." He felt discouraged and imagined her the adored partner of some young doctor, a brilliant surgeon perhaps, with whom she shared many professional interests. His last impression as the elevator doors closed to take

him to street level was that of Miss Hill walking
down the corridor, chatting animatedly with the
other nurse, her hips swinging seductively and her
laugh musically beautiful as it pierced the grim
hush of the ward. I must have her, Mendel
thought, consumed by longing and passion, and
I must not blow it like I have so many others in
the past. I must proceed sensibly. Not too fast as
is always my problem. I must not act precipi-
tously. I must find out more about her. Is she
indeed as wonderful as I imagine she is? And if
so, how committed is she to the other person?
And if he didn't exist, would I even then have a
chance? I see no reason why if she's free that I
couldn't court her and win her. Or even win her
from this man. But I need time. Time to learn
about her. Then time to work on her. To talk, to
laugh, to bring what gifts I have of insight and
humor to bear. Mendel was practically wringing
his palms like a Medici prince and drooling. The
logical plan is to see her as I visit Iskowitz and
slowly, without pressing, build up points with her.
I must be oblique. My hard sell, direct approach
has failed me too often in the past. I must be
restrained.

This decided, Mendel came to see Iskowitz
every day. The patient couldn't believe his good
fortune to have such a devoted friend. Mendel
always brought a substantial and well thought
out gift. One that would help him make a score
in the eyes of Miss Hill. Pretty flowers, a biogra-
phy of Tolstoy (he heard her mention how much

she loved *Anna Karenina*), the poetry of Wordsworth, caviar. Iskowitz was stunned by the
choices. He hated caviar and never heard of
Wordsworth. Mendel did stop short of bringing
Iskowitz a pair of antique earrings although he
saw some he knew Miss Hill would adore.

The smitten suitor seized every opportunity to
engage Iskowitz's nurse in conversation. Yes, she
was engaged, he learned, but had trepidations
about it. Her fiancé was a lawyer but she had fantasies of marrying someone more in the arts. Still,
Norman, her beau, was tall and dark and gor-
geous, a description that left the less physically
prepossessing Mendel in a discouraged state.
Mendel would always trumpet his accomplish-
ments and observations to the deteriorating Iskowitz, in a voice loud enough to be heard by Miss
Hill. He sensed that he might be impressing her
but each time his position appeared strong, future
plans with Norman entered the conversation. How
lucky is this Norman, Mendel thought. He spends
time with her, they laugh together, plan, he
presses his lips to hers, he removes her nurse's
uniform—perhaps not every stitch of it. Oh God!
Mendel sighed, looking heavenward and shaking
his head in frustration.

"You have no idea what these visits mean to
Mr. Iskowitz," the nurse told Mendel one day, her
delightful smile and big eyes making him go a
hundred. "He has no family and most of his other
friends have so little free time. My theory is, of
course, that most people don't have the compas-

sion or courage to spend lots of time with a terminal case. People write off the dying patient and prefer not to think about it. That's why I think your behavior is—well—magnificent."

Word of Mendel's indulgence of Iskowitz got around and at the weekly card game he was much beloved by the players.

"What you're doing is wonderful," Phil Birnbaum said to Mendel over poker. "Meyer tells me no one comes as regularly as you do and he says he thinks you even dress up for the occasion." Mendel's mind was fixed at that second on Miss Hill's hips, which he couldn't get out of his thoughts.

"So how is he? Is he brave?" Sol Katz asked.

"Is who brave?" Mendel asked in his reverie.

"Who? Who we talking about? Poor Meyer."

"Oh, er—yeah. Brave. Right," Mendel said, not even realizing he was at that moment holding a full house.

As the weeks passed, Iskowitz wasted away. Once, in a weakened condition, he looked up at Mendel who stood over him and muttered, "Lenny, I love you. Really." Mendel took Meyer's outstretched hand and said, "Thanks, Meyer. Listen, was Miss Hill in today? Huh? Could you speak up a little? It's hard to understand you." Iskowitz nodded weakly. "Uh-huh," Mendel said, "so what'd you guys talk about? Did my name come up?"

Mendel, of course, had not dared make a move for Miss Hill, finding himself in the awkward position of not wanting her ever to dream that he was there so frequently for any reason other than to see Meyer Iskowitz.

Sometimes, being at death's door would inspire the patient to philosophize and he would say things like, "We're here, we don't know why. It's over before we know what hit us. The trick is to enjoy the moment. To be alive is to be happy. And yet I believe God exists and when I look around me and see the sunlight streaming through the window or the stars come out at night, I know that He has some ultimate plan and that it's good."

"Right, right," Mendel would answer. "And Miss Hill? Is she still seeing Norman? Did you find out what I asked you? If you see her when they come to do those tests on you tomorrow, find out."

On a rainy April day Iskowitz died. Before expiring he told Mendel once again that he loved him and that Mendel's concern for him in these last months was the most touching and deepest experience he ever had with another human being. Two weeks later Miss Hill and Norman broke up and Mendel started dating her. They had an affair that lasted a year and then they went their separate ways.

"That's some story," Moscowitz said when Koppelman finished relating this tale about the shallowness of Lenny Mendel. "It goes to show how some people are just no damn good."

"I didn't get that out of it," Jake Fishbein said.

"Not at all. The story shows how love of a woman enables a man to overcome his fears of mortality if only for a while."

"What are you talking about?" Abe Trochman chimed in. "The point of the story is that a dying man becomes the beneficiary of his friend's sudden adoration of a woman."

"But they weren't friends," Lupowitz argued. "Mendel went out of obligation. He returned out of self-interest."

"What's the difference?" Trochman said. "Iskowitz experienced a closeness. He died comforted. That it was motivated by Mendel's lust for the nurse—so?"

"Lust? Who said lust? Mendel, despite his shallowness, may have felt love for the first time in his life."

"What's the difference?" Bursky said. "Who cares what the point of the story is? If it even has a point. It was an entertaining anecdote. Let's order."

The Query

(The following is a one-act play based on an incident in the life of Abraham Lincoln. The incident may or may not be true. The point is I was tired when I wrote it.)

I

(Lincoln with boyish eagerness beckons George Jennings, his press secretary, into the room.)

Jennings: Mr. Lincoln, you sent for me?

Lincoln: Yes, Jennings. Come in. Sit down.

Jennings: Yes, Mr. President?

Lincoln: (Unable to suppress a grin) I want to discuss an idea.

Jennings: Of course, sir.

Lincoln: Next time we have a conference for the gentlemen of the press . . .

Jennings: Yessir . . . ?

Lincoln: When I take questions . . .

Jennings: Yes, Mr. President . . . ?

Lincoln: You raise your hand and ask me: Mr. President, how long do you think a man's legs should be?

Jennings: Pardon me?

Lincoln: You ask me: how long do I think a man's legs should be?

Jennings: May I ask why, sir?

Lincoln: Why? Because I have a very good answer.

Jennings: You do?

Lincoln: Long enough to reach the ground.

Jennings: Excuse me?

Lincoln: Long enough to reach the ground. That's the answer! Get it? How long do you think a man's legs should be? Long enough to reach the ground!

Jennings: I see.

Lincoln: You don't think it's funny?

Jennings: May I be frank, Mr. President?

Lincoln: (Annoyed) Well, I got a big laugh with it today.

Jennings: Really?

Lincoln: Absolutely. I was with the cabinet and some friends and a man asked it and I shot back that answer and the whole room broke up.

Jennings: May I ask, Mr. Lincoln, in what context did he ask it?

Lincoln: Pardon me?

Jennings: Were you discussing anatomy? Was the man a surgeon or a sculptor?

Lincoln: Why-er-no-I-I-don't think so. No. A simple farmer, I believe.

Jennings: Well, why did he want to know?

Lincoln: Well, I don't know. All I know is he was someone who had requested an audience with me urgently . . .

Jennings: (Concerned) I see.

Lincoln: What is it, Jennings, you look pale?

Jennings: It is a rather odd question.

Lincoln: Yes, but I got a laugh off it. It was a quick answer.

Jennings: No one's denying that, Mr. Lincoln.

Lincoln: A big laugh. The whole cabinet just broke up.

Jennings: And then did the man say anything?

Lincoln: He said thank you and left.

Jennings: You never asked why he wanted to know?

Lincoln: If you must know, I was too pleased with my answer. Long enough to reach the ground. It came out so fast. I didn't hesitate.

Jennings: I know, I know. It's just, well, this whole thing's got me worried.

II

(Lincoln and Mary Todd in their bedroom, middle of the night. She in bed, Lincoln pacing nervously.)

Mary: Come to bed, Abe. What's wrong?

Lincoln: That man today. The question. I can't get it out of my mind. Jennings's opened a can of worms.

Mary: Forget it, Abe.

Lincoln: I want to, Mary. Jesus, don't you think I want to? But those haunting eyes. Imploring. What could have prompted it? I need a drink.

Mary: No, Abe.

Lincoln: Yes.

Mary: I said, no! You've been jittery lately. It's this damn civil war.

Lincoln: It's not the war. I didn't respond to the human being. I was too preoccupied with getting the quick laugh. I allowed a complex issue to elude me just so I could get some chuckles from my cabinet. They hate me anyhow.

Mary: They love you, Abe.

Lincoln: I'm vain. Still, it was a fast comeback.

Mary: I agree. Your answer was clever. Long enough to reach his torso.

Lincoln: To reach the ground.

Mary: No, you said it the other way.

Lincoln: No. What's funny about that?

Mary: To me it's a lot funnier.

Lincoln: That's funnier?

Mary: Sure.

Lincoln: Mary, you don't know what you're talking about.

Mary: The image of legs rising to a torso . . .

Lincoln: Forget it! Can we forget it! Where's the bourbon?

Mary: (Withholding the bottle) No, Abe. You won't drink tonight! I won't allow it!

Lincoln: Mary, what's happened to us? We used to have such fun.

Mary: (*Tenderly*) Come here, Abe. There's a full moon tonight. Like the night we met.

Lincoln: No, Mary. The night we met there was a waning moon.

Mary: Full.

Lincoln: Waning.

Mary: Full.

Lincoln: I'll get the almanac.

Mary: Oh Christ, Abe, forget it!

Lincoln: I'm sorry.

Mary: Is it the question? The legs? Is it still that?

Lincoln: What did he mean?

III

(*The cabin of Will Haines and his wife. Haines enters after a long ride. Alice puts down her quilting basket and runs to him.*)

Alice: Well, did you ask him? Will he pardon Andrew?

Will: (*Beside himself*) Oh, Alice, I did such a stupid thing.

Side Effects

Alice: (Bitterly) What? Don't tell me he won't pardon our son?

Will: I didn't ask him.

Alice: You what!? You didn't ask him!?

Will: I don't know what came over me. There he was, the President of the United States, surrounded by important people. His cabinet, his friends. Then someone said, Mr. Lincoln, this man has ridden all day to speak to you. He has a question to ask. All the while I was riding I had gone over the question in my mind. "Mr. Lincoln, sir, our boy Andrew made a mistake. I realize how serious it is to fall asleep on guard duty, but executing such a young man seems so cruel. Mr. President, sir, couldn't you commute his sentence?"

Alice: That was the correct way to put it.

Will: But for some reason, with all those folks staring at me, when the President said, "Yes, what is your question?" I said, "Mr. Lincoln, how long do you think a man's legs should be?"

Alice: What?

Will: That's right. That was my question. Don't ask me why it came out. How long do you think a man's legs should be?

Alice: What kind of question is that?

Will: I'm telling you, I don't know.

Alice: His legs? How long?

Will: Oh, Alice, forgive me.

Alice: How long should a man's legs be? That's the stupidest question I've ever heard.

Will: I know, I know. Don't keep reminding me.

Alice: But why leg length? I mean, legs are not a subject that particularly interests you.

Will: I was fumfering for words. I forgot my original request. I could hear the clock ticking. I didn't want to appear tongue-tied.

Alice: Did Mr. Lincoln say anything? Did he answer?

Will: Yes. He said, long enough to reach the ground.

Alice: Long enough to reach the ground? What the hell does that mean?

Will: Who knows? But he got a big laugh. Of course, those guys are disposed toward reacting.

Alice: (Suddenly turns) Maybe you really didn't want Andrew pardoned.

Will: What?

Alice: Maybe down deep you don't want our son's sentence commuted. Maybe you're jealous of him.

Will: You're crazy. I-I. Me? Jealous?

Alice: Why not? He's stronger. He's smoother with pick and ax and hoe. He's got a feel for the soil like no man I've seen.

Will: Stop it! Stop it!

Alice: Let's face it, William, you're a lousy farmer.

Will: (Trembling with panic) Yes, I admit it! I hate farming! The seeds all look alike to me! And the soil! I can never tell it apart from dirt! You, from the east, with your fancy schools! Laughing at me. Sneering. I plant turnips and corn comes up! You think that doesn't hurt a man!?

Alice: If you would just fasten the seed packets to a little stick you'd know what you planted!

Will: I want to die! Everything is going black!

The Query

(Suddenly there is a knock at the door and when Alice opens it, it is none other than Abraham Lincoln. He is haggard and red-eyed.)

Lincoln: Mr. Haines?

Will: President Lincoln . . .

Lincoln: That question—

Will: I know, I know . . . how stupid of me! It was all I could think of, I was so nervous.

(Haines falls on his knees weeping. Lincoln also weeps.)

Lincoln: Then I was right. It was a non sequitur.

Will: Yes, yes . . . forgive me . . .

Lincoln: (Weeping unashamedly) I do, I do. Rise. Stand up. Your boy will be pardoned today. As will all boys who made a mistake be forgiven.

(Gathering the Haines family in his arms)

Your stupid question has caused me to reevaluate my life. For that I thank you and love you.

Alice: We did some reevaluating too, Abe. May we call you . . . ?

Lincoln: Yes, sure, why not? Do you guys have anything to eat? A man travels so many miles, at least offer him something.

(As they break out the bread and cheese the curtain falls.)

Fabrizio's:
Criticism and
Response

(An exchange in one of the more thought-provoking journals, in which Fabian Plotnick, our most high-minded restaurant critic, reviews Fabrizio's Villa Nova Restaurant, on Second Avenue, and, as usual, stimulates some profound responses.)

PASTA AS AN expression of Italian Neo-Realistic starch is well understood by Mario Spinelli, the chef at Fabrizio's. Spinelli kneads his pasta slowly. He allows a buildup of tension by the customers as they sit salivating. His fettuccine, though wry and puckish in an almost mischievous way, owes a lot to Barzino, whose use of fettuccine as an instrument of social change is known to us all. The difference is that at Barzino's the patron is led to expect white fettuccine and gets it. Here at Fabrizio's he gets green fettuccine. Why? It all seems so gratuitous. As customers, we are not prepared for the change. Hence, the

173

green noodle does not amuse us. It's disconcerting in a way unintended by the chef. The linguine, on the other hand, is quite delicious and not at all didactic. True, there is a pervasive Marxist quality to it, but this is hidden by the sauce. Spinelli has been a devoted Italian Communist for years, and has had great success in espousing his Marxism by subtly including it in the tortellini.

I began my meal with an antipasto, which at first appeared aimless, but as I focused more on the anchovies the point of it became clearer. Was Spinelli trying to say that all life was represented here in this antipasto, with the black olives an unbearable reminder of mortality? If so, where was the celery? Was the omission deliberate? At Jacobelli's, the antipasto consists solely of celery. But Jacobelli is an extremist. He wants to call our attention to the absurdity of life. Who can forget his scampi: four garlic-drenched shrimp arranged in a way that says more about our involvement in Vietnam than countless books on the subject? What an outrage in its time! Now it appears tame next to Gino Finochi's (of Gino's Vesuvio Restaurant) Soft Piccata, a startling six-foot slice of veal with a piece of black chiffon attached to it. (Finochi always works better in veal than either fish or chicken, and it was a shocking oversight by *Time* when reference to him was omitted in the cover story on Robert Rauschenberg.) Spinelli, unlike these avant-garde chefs, rarely goes all the way. He hesitates, as with his spumoni, and when it comes, of course it is melted. There has always been a certain tentativeness about Spinelli's style—particularly in his treatment of Spaghetti Vongole. (Before his psychoanalysis, clams held great terror for Spinelli. He could not bear to open them, and when forced to look inside he blacked out. His early attempts at Vongole saw him dealing exclusively with "clam substitutes." He used peanuts, olives, and finally, before his breakdown, little rubber erasers.)

One lovely touch at Fabrizio's is Spinelli's Boneless Chicken Parmigiana. The title is ironic, for he has filled the chicken with extra bones, as if to say life must not be ingested too quickly or without caution. The constant removal of bones from the mouth and the depositing of them on the plate give the meal an eerie sound. One is reminded at once of Webern, who seems to crop up all the time in Spinelli's cooking. Robert Craft, writing about Stravinsky, makes an interesting point about Schoenberg's influence on Spinelli's salads and Spinelli's influence on Stravinsky's Concerto in D for Strings. In point of fact, the minestrone is a great example of atonality. Cluttered as it is with odd bits and pieces of food, the customer is forced to make noises with his mouth as he drinks it. These tones are arranged in a set pattern and repeat themselves in serial order. The first night I was at Fabrizio's, two patrons, a young boy and a fat man, were drinking soup simultaneously, and the excitement was such that they received a standing ovation. For dessert, we had tortoni, and I was reminded of Leibniz's remarkable pronouncement: "The Monads have no windows." How apropos! Fabrizio's prices, as Hannah Arendt told me once, are "reasonable without being historically inevitable." I agree.

To the Editors:
Fabian Plotnick's insights into Fabrizio's Villa Nova Restaurant are full of merit and perspicuity. The only point missing from his penetrating analysis is that while Fabrizio's is a family-run restaurant, it does not conform to the classic Italian nuclear-family structure but, curiously, is modeled on the homes of pre-Industrial Revolution middle-class Welsh miners. Fabrizio's relationships with his wife and sons are capitalistic and peer-group oriented. The sexual mores of the help are typically Victorian—especially the girl who runs the cash register. Working conditions also reflect English factory problems, and waiters are often made to serve eight to ten hours a day with napkins that do not meet current safety standards.

Dove Rapkin

To the Editors:
In his review of Fabrizio's Villa Nova, Fabian Plotnick called the prices "reasonable." But would he call Eliot's Four Quartets "reasonable"? Eliot's return to a more primitive stage of the Logos doctrine reflects immanent reason in the world, but $8.50 for chicken tetrazzini! It doesn't make sense, even in a Catholic context. I refer Mr. Plot-

nick to the article in *Encounter* (2/58) entitled "Eliot, Reincarnation, and Zuppa Di Clams."

Eino Shmeederer

To the Editors:
What Mr. Plotnick fails to take into account in discussing Mario Spinelli's fettuccine is, of course, the size of the portions, or, to put it more directly, the quantity of the noodles. There are obviously as many odd-numbered noodles as all the odd- and even-numbered noodles combined. (Clearly a paradox.) The logic breaks down linguistically, and consequently Mr. Plotnick cannot use the word "fettuccine" with any accuracy. Fettuccine becomes a symbol; that is to say, let the fettuccine $= x$. Then $a = x/b$ (b standing for a constant equal to half of any entrée). By this logic, one would have to say: the fettuccine *is* the linguine! How ridiculous. The sentence clearly cannot be stated as "The fettuccine was delicious." It must be stated as "The fettuccine and the linguine are not the rigatoni." As Gödel declared over and over, "Everything must be translated into logical calculus before being eaten."

Prof. Word Babcocke
Massachusetts Institute of Technology

To the Editors:
I have read with great interest Mr. Fabian Plotnick's review of Fabrizio's Villa Nova, and find it to be yet another shocking contemporary example of revisionist history. How quickly we forget

that during the worst era of the Stalinist purges Fabrizio's not only was open for business but enlarged its back room to seat more customers! No one there said anything about Soviet political repression. In fact, when the Committee to Free Soviet Dissidents petitioned Fabrizio's to leave the gnocchi off the menu until the Russians freed Gregor Tomshinsky, the well-known Trotskyite short-order cook, they refused. Tomshinsky by then had compiled ten thousand pages of recipes, all of which were confiscated by the N.K.V.D.

"Contributing to the heartburn of a minor" was the pathetic excuse the Soviet court used to send Tomshinsky into forced labor. Where were all the so-called intellectuals at Fabrizio's then? The coat-check girl, Tina, never made the smallest attempt to raise her voice when coat-check girls all over the Soviet Union were taken from their homes and forced to hang up clothing for Stalinist hoodlums. I might add that when dozens of Soviet physicists were accused of overeating and then jailed, many restaurants closed in protest, but Fabrizio's kept up its usual service and even instituted the policy of giving free after-dinner mints! I myself ate at Fabrizio's in the thirties, and saw that it was a hotbed of dyed-in-the-wool Stalinists who tried to serve blinchiki to unsuspecting souls who ordered pasta. To say that most customers did not know what was going on in the kitchen is absurd. When somebody ordered scungilli and was handed a blintz, it was quite clear what was happening. The truth is, the intellectuals simply preferred not to see the difference. I dined there once with Professor Gideon Cheops, who was served an entire Russian meal, consisting of borscht, Chicken Kiev, and halvah—upon which he said to me, "Isn't this spaghetti wonderful?"

Prof. Quincy Mondragon
New York University

Fabian Plotnick *replies:*
Mr. Shmeederer shows he knows nothing of either restaurant prices or the "Four Quartets." Eliot himself felt $7.50 for good chicken tetrazzini was (I quote from an interview in *Partisan Review*) "not out of line." Indeed, in "The Dry Salvages," Eliot imputes this very notion to Krishna, though not precisely in those words.

I'm grateful to Dove Rapkin for his comments on the nuclear family, and also to Professor Babcocke for his penetrating linguistic analysis, although I question his equation and suggest, rather, the following model:

(a) some pasta is linguine
(b) all linguine is not spaghetti
(c) no spaghetti is pasta, hence all spaghetti is linguine.

Wittgenstein used the above model to prove the existence of God, and later Bertrand Russell used it to prove that not only does God exist but He found Wittgenstein too short.

Finally, to Professor Mondragon. It is true that Spinelli worked in the kitchen of Fabrizio's in the nineteen-thirties—perhaps longer than he should have. Yet it is certainly to his credit that when the infamous House Un-American Activities Committee pressured him to change the wording on his menus from "Prosciutto and melon" to the less politically sensitive "Prosciutto and figs," he took the case to the Supreme Court and forced the now famous ruling "Appetizers are entitled to full protection under the First Amendment."

Retribution

THAT CONNIE CHASEN returned my fatal attraction toward her at first sight was a miracle unparalleled in the history of Central Park West. Tall, blond, high cheekboned, an actress, a scholar, a charmer, irrevocably alienated, with a hostile and perceptive wit only challenged in its power to attract by the lewd, humid eroticism her every curve suggested, she was the unrivaled desideratum of each young man at the party. That she would settle on me, Harold Cohen, scrawny, long-nosed, twenty-four-year-old, budding dramatist and whiner, was a *non sequitur* on a par with octuplets. True, I have a facile way with a one-liner and seem able to keep a conversation going on a wide range of topics, and yet I was taken by surprise that this superbly scaled apparition could zero in on my meager gifts so rapidly and completely.

"You're adorable," she told me, after an hour's

energetic exchange while we leaned against a bookcase, throwing back Valpolicella and finger foods. "I hope you're going to call me."

"Call you? I'd like to go home with you right now."

"Well great," she said, smiling coquettishly. "The truth is, I didn't really think I was impressing you."

I affected a casual air while blood pounded through my arteries to predictable destinations. I blushed, an old habit.

"I think you're dynamite," I said, causing her to glow even more incandescently. Actually I was quite unprepared for such immediate acceptance. My grape-fueled cockiness was an attempt to lay groundwork for the future, so that when I would indeed suggest the boudoir, let's say, one discreet date later, it would not come as a total surprise and violate some tragically established Platonic bond. Yet, cautious, guilt-ridden, worrier-victim that I am, this night was to be mine. Connie Chasen and I had taken to each other in a way that would not be denied and one brief hour later were thrashing balletically through the percales, executing with total emotional commitment the absurd choreography of human passion. To me, it was the most erotic and satisfying night of sex I had ever had, and as she lay in my arms afterward, relaxed and fulfilled, I wondered exactly how Fate was going to extract its inevitable dues. Would I soon go blind? Or become a paraplegic? What hideous vigorish would Harold Cohen be forced to pony up so the cosmos might continue in its harmonious rounds? But this would all come later.

The following four weeks burst no bubbles. Connie and I explored one another and delighted in each new discovery. I found her quick, exciting, and responsive; her imagination was fertile and her references erudite and varied. She could discuss Novalis and quote from the Rig-Veda. The verse of every song by Cole Porter, she knew by heart. In bed she was uninhibited and experimental, a true child of the future. On the minus side one had to be niggling to find fault. True she could be a tad temperamental. She inevitably changed her food order in a restaurant and always long after it was decent to do so. Invariably she got angry when I pointed out this was not exactly fair to waiter or chef. Also she switched diets every other day, committing with whole heart to one and then disregarding it in favor of some new, fashionable theory on weight loss. Not that she was remotely overweight. Quite the opposite. Her shape would have been the envy of a *Vogue* model, and yet an inferiority complex rivaling Franz Kafka's led her to painful bouts of self-criticism. To hear her tell it, she was a dumpy little nonentity, who had no business trying to be an actress, much less attempting Chekhov. My assurances were moderately encouraging and I kept them flowing, though I felt that if her desirability was not apparent from my obsessional glee over her brain and body, no amount of talk would be convincing.

Along about the sixth week of a wonderful romance, her insecurity emerged full blown one day. Her parents were having a barbecue in Connecticut and I was at last going to meet her family.

"Dad's great," she said worshipfully, "and great-looking. And Mom's beautiful. Are yours?"

"I wouldn't say beautiful," I confessed. Actually, I had a rather dim view of my family's physical appearance, likening the relatives on my mother's side to something usually cultured in a petri dish. I was very hard on my family and we all constantly teased each other and fought, but were close. Indeed, a compliment had not passed through the lips of any member during my lifetime and I suspect not since God made his covenant with Abraham.

"My folks never fight," she said. "They drink, but they're real polite. And Danny's nice." Her brother. "I mean he's strange but sweet. He writes music."

"I'm looking forward to meeting them all."

"I hope you don't fall for my kid sister, Lindsay."

"Oh sure."

"She's two years younger than me and so bright and sexy. Everyone goes nuts over her."

"Sounds impressive," I said. Connie stroked my face.

"I hope you don't like her better than me," she

said in half-serious tones that enabled her to voice this fear gracefully.

"I wouldn't worry," I assured her.

"No? Promise?"

"Are you two competitive?"

"No. We love each other. But she's got an angel's face and a sexy, round body. She takes after Mom. And she's got this real high IQ and great sense of humor."

"You're beautiful," I said and kissed her. But I must admit, for the rest of that day, fantasies of twenty-one-year-old Lindsay Chasen did not leave my mind. Good Lord, I thought, what if she is this *Wunderkind?* What if she is indeed as irresistible as Connie paints her? Might I not be smitten? Weakling that I am, might not the sweet body scent and tinkling laugh of a stunning Connecticut WASP named Lindsay—Lindsay yet!— not turn this fascinated, though unpledged, head from Connie toward fresh mischief? After all, I had only known Connie six weeks and, while having a wonderful time with the woman, was not yet actually in love with her beyond all reason. Still, Lindsay would have to be pretty damn fabulous to cause a ripple in the giddy tempest of chuckles and lust that made these past three fortnights such a spree.

That evening I made love with Connie, but when I slept it was Lindsay who trespassed my dreams. Sweet little Lindsay, the adorable Phi Beta Kappa with the face of a movie star and the charm of a princess. I tossed and turned and woke in the middle of the night with a strange feeling of excitement and foreboding.

In the morning my fantasies subsided, and after breakfast Connie and I set off for Connecticut bearing wine and flowers. We drove through the fall countryside listening to Vivaldi on FM and exchanging our observations on that day's Arts and Leisure Section. Then, moments before we passed through the front gate of the Chasens' Lyme acreage, I once again wondered if I was about to be stupefied by this formidable kid sister.

"Will Lindsay's boyfriend be here?" I asked in a probing, guilt-strangled falsetto.

"They're finished," Connie explained. "Lindsay runs through one a month. She's a heartbreaker." Hmm, I thought, in addition to all else, the young woman is available. Might she really be more exciting than Connie? I found it hard to believe, and yet I tried to prepare myself for any eventuality. Any, of course, except the one that occurred that crisp, clear, Sunday afternoon.

Connie and I joined the barbecue, where there was much revelry and drinking. I met the family, one by one, scattered as they were amidst their fashionable, attractive cohorts and though sister Lindsay was indeed all Connie had described— comely, flirtatious, and fun to talk to—I did not prefer her to Connie. Of the two, I still felt much more taken with the older sister than the twenty-one-year-old Vassar grad. No, the one I hopelessly lost my heart to that day was none other than Connie's fabulous mother, Emily.

Emily Chasen, fifty-five, buxom, tanned, a ravishing pioneer face with pulled-back greying hair and round, succulent curves that expressed themselves in flawless arcs like a Brancusi. Sexy Emily, whose huge, white smile and chesty, big laugh combined to create an irresistible warmth and seductiveness.

What protoplasm in this family, I thought! What award-winning genes! Consistent genes too, as Emily Chasen seemed to be as at ease with me as her daughter was. Clearly she enjoyed talking with me as I monopolized her time, mindless of the demands of the other afternoon guests. We discussed photography (her hobby) and books. She was currently reading, with great delight, a book of Joseph Heller's. She found it hilarious and laughing fetchingly as she filled my glass said, "God, you Jews are truly exotic." Exotic? She should only know the Greenblatts. Or Mr and Mrs Milton Sharpstein, my father's friends. Or for that matter, my cousin Tovah. Exotic? I mean, they're nice but hardly exotic with their endless bickering over the best way to combat indigestion or how far back to sit from the television set.

Emily and I talked for hours of movies, and we discussed my hopes for the theatre and her new interest in making collages. Obviously this woman had many creative and intellectual demands that for one reason or another remained pent up within her. Yet clearly she was not unhappy with her life as she and her husband, John Chasen, an older version of the man you'd like to have piloting your plane, hugged and drank in lovey-dovey fashion. Indeed, in comparison to my own folks, who had been married inexplicably for forty years (out of spite it seemed), Emily and John seemed like the Lunts. My folks, naturally, could not discuss even the weather without accusations and recriminations just short of gunfire.

When it came time to go home I was quite sorry and left with dreams of Emily in complete command of my thoughts.

"They're sweet, aren't they?" Connie asked as we sped toward Manhattan.

"Very," I concurred.

"Isn't Dad a knockout? He's really fun."

"Umm." The truth was I had hardly exchanged ten sentences with Connie's dad.

"And Mom looked great today. Better than in a long time. She's been ill with the flu, too."

"She's quite something," I said.

"Her photography and collages are very good," Connie said. "I wish Dad encouraged her more instead of being so old-fashioned. He's just not fascinated by creativity in the arts. Never was."

"Too bad," I said. "I hope it hasn't been too frustrating for your mother over the years."

"It has," Connie said. "And Lindsay? Are you in love with her?"

"She's lovely—but not in your class. At least as far as I'm concerned."

"I'm relieved," Connie said laughingly and pecked me on the cheek. Abysmal vermin that I am, I couldn't, of course, tell her that it was her incredible mother that I wanted to see again. Yet even as I drove, my mind clicked and blinked like a computer in hopes of concocting some scheme to filch more time with this overpowering and wonderful woman. If you had asked me where I expected it to lead, I really couldn't have said. I knew only as I drove through the cold, night, autumn air that somewhere Freud, Sophocles, and Eugene O'Neill were laughing.

During the next several months I managed to see Emily Chasen many times. Usually it was in an innocent threesome with Connie, both of us meeting her in the city and taking her to a museum or concert. Once or twice I did something with Emily alone if Connie was busy. This delighted Connie—that her mother and lover should be such good friends. Once or twice I contrived to be where Emily was "by accident" and wound up having an apparently impromptu walk or drink with her. It was obvious she enjoyed my company as I listened sympathetically to her artistic aspirations and laughed engagingly at her jokes. Together we discussed music and literature and life, my observations consistently entertaining her. It was also obvious the idea of regarding me as anything more than just a new friend was not remotely on her mind. Or if it was, she certainly never let on. Yet what could I expect? I was living with her daughter. Cohabiting honorably in a civilized society where certain taboos are observed. After all, who did I imagine this woman was anyhow? Some amoral vamp out of German films who would seduce her own child's lover? In truth, I'm sure I would have lost all respect for her if she did confess feelings for me or behave in any other way than untouchable. And yet I had a terrible crush on her. It amounted to genuine longing, and despite all logic I prayed for some tiny hint that her marriage was not as perfect as it seemed or that, resist as she might, she had grown fatally fond of me. There were times that I flirted with the notion of making some tepidly aggressive move myself, but banner headlines in the yellow press formed in my mind and I shrank from any action.

I wanted so badly, in my anguish, to explain these confused feelings to Connie in an above-board way and enlist her aid in making sense out of the painful tangle, but I felt to do so invited certain carnage. In fact, instead of this manly honesty, I nosed around like a ferret for bits and clues regarding Emily's feelings toward me.

"I took your mother to the Matisse exhibit," I said to Connie one day.

"I know," she said. "She had a great time."

"She's a lucky woman. Seems to be happy. Fine marriage."

"Yes." Pause.

"So, er—did she say anything to you?"

"She said you two had a wonderful talk afterwards. About her photography."

"Right." Pause. "Anything else? About me? I mean, I felt maybe I get overbearing."

"Oh God, no. She adores you."

"Yes?"

"With Danny spending more and more time with Dad, she thinks of you kind of like a son."

"Her son!?" I said, shattered.

"I think she would have liked a son who is as interested in her work as you are. A genuine companion. More intellectually inclined than Danny. Sensitive to her artistic needs a little. I think you fulfill that role for her."

That night I was in a foul mood and, as I sat home with Connie watching television, my body again ached to be pressed in passionate tenderness against this woman who apparently thought of me as nothing more dangerous than her boy. Or did she? Was this not just a casual surmise of Connie's? Might Emily not be thrilled to find out that a man, much younger than herself, found her beautiful and sexy and fascinating and longed to have an affair with her quite unlike anything remotely filial? Wasn't it possible a woman of that age, particularly one whose husband was not overly responsive to her deepest feelings, would welcome the attention of a passionate admirer? And might I not, mired in my own middle-class background, be making too much of the fact that I was living with her daughter? After all, stranger things happen. Certainly amongst temperaments gifted with profounder artistic intensity. I had to resolve matters and finally put an end to these feelings which had assumed the proportions of a mad obsession. The situation was taking too heavy a toll on me, and it was time I either acted on it or put it out of my mind. I decided to act.

Past successful campaigns suggested instantly the proper route to take. I would steer her to Trader Vic's, that dimly lit, foolproof Polynesian den of delights where dark, promising corners abounded and deceptively mild rum drinks quickly unchained the fiery libido from its dungeon. A pair of Mai Tai's and it would be anybody's ball game. A hand on the knee. A sudden uninhibited kiss. Fingers intertwined. The miraculous booze would work its dependable magic. It had never failed me in the past. Even when the unsuspecting victim pulled back with eyebrows arched, one could back out gracefully by imputing all to the effects of the island brew.

"Forgive me," I could alibi, "I'm just so zonked by this drink. I don't know what I'm doing."

Yes, the time for polite chitchat was over, I thought. I am in love with two women, a not terribly uncommon problem. That they happen to be mother and child? All the more challenging! I was becoming hysterical. Yet drunk with confidence as I was at that point, I must admit that things did not finally come off quite as planned. True, we did make it to Trader Vic's one cold February afternoon. We did also look in each other's eyes and waxed poetic about life while knocking back tall, foamy, white beverages that held minuscule wooden parasols lanced into floating pineapple squares—but there it ended. And it did so because, despite the unblocking of my baser urges, I felt that it would completely destroy Connie. In the end it was my own guilty conscience—or, more accurately, my return to sanity—that prevented me from placing the predictable hand on Emily Chasen's leg and pursuing my dark desires. That sudden realization that I was only a mad fantasizer who, in fact, loved Connie and must never risk hurting her in any way did me in. Yes, Harold Cohen was a more conventional type than he would have us believe. And more in love with his girl friend than he cared to admit. This crush on Emily Chasen would have to be filed and forgotten. Painful as it might be to control my impulses toward Connie's mom, rationality and decent consideration would prevail.

After a wonderful afternoon, the crowning moment of which would have been the ferocious kissing of Emily's large, inviting lips, I got the check and called it a day. We exited laughingly into the lightly blowing snow and, after walking her to her car, I watched her take off for Lyme while I returned home to her daughter with a new, deeper feeling of warmth for this woman who nightly shared my bed. Life is truly chaos, I thought. Feelings are so unpredictable. How does anyone ever stay married for forty years? This, it seems, is more of a miracle than the parting of the Red Sea, though my father, in his naïveté, holds the latter to be a greater achievement. I kissed Connie and confessed the depth of my affection. She reciprocated. We made love.

Dissolve, as they say in the movies, to a few

months later. Connie can no longer have inter-course with me. And why? I brought it on myself like the tragic protagonist of a Greek play. Our sex began falling off insidiously weeks ago.

"What's wrong?" I'd ask. "Have I done something?"

"God no, it's not your fault. Oh hell."

"What? Tell me."

"I'm just not up to it," she'd say. "Must we *every* night?" The every night she referred to was in actuality only a few nights a week and soon less than that.

"I can't," she'd say guiltily when I'd attempt to instigate sex. "You know I'm going through a bad time."

"What bad time?" I asked incredulously. "Are you seeing someone else?"

"Of course not."

"Do you love me?"

"Yes. I wish I didn't."

"So what? Why the turnoff? And it's not getting better, it's getting worse."

"I can't do it with you," she confessed one night. "You remind me of my brother."

"What?"

"You remind me of Danny. Don't ask me why."

"Your brother? You must be joking!"

"No."

"But he's a twenty-three-year-old, blond WASP who works in your father's law practice, and I remind you of him?"

"It's like going to bed with my brother," she wept.

"O.K., O.K., don't cry. We'll be all right. I have to take some aspirin and lie down. I don't feel well." I pressed my throbbing temples and pretended to be bewildered, but it was, of course, obvious that my strong relationship with her mother had in some way cast me in a fraternal role as far as Connie was concerned. Fate was getting even. I was to be tortured like Tantalus, inches from the svelte, tanned body of Connie Chasen, yet unable to lay a hand on her without, at least for the time being, eliciting the classical expletive, "Yuck." In the irrational assigning of parts that occurs in all of our emotional dramas, I had suddenly become a sibling.

Various stages of anguish marked the next months. First the pain of being rejected in bed. Next, telling ourselves the condition was temporary. This was accompanied by an attempt by me to be understanding, to be patient. I recalled not being able to perform with a sexy date in college once precisely because some vague twist of her head reminded me of my Aunt Rifka. This girl was far prettier than the squirrel-faced aunt of my boyhood, but the notion of making love with my mother's sister wrecked the moment irreparably. I knew what Connie was going through, and yet sexual frustration mounted and compounded itself. After a time, my self-control sought expression in sarcastic remarks and later in an urge to burn down the house. Still, I kept trying not to be rash, trying to ride out the storm of unreason and preserve what in all other ways was a good relationship with Connie. My suggestion for her to see a psychoanalyst fell on deaf ears, as nothing was more alien to her Connecticut up-bringing than the Jewish science from Vienna.

"Sleep with other women. What else can I say?" she offered.

"I don't want to sleep with other women. I love you."

"And I love you. You know that. But I can't go to bed with you." Indeed I was not the type who slept around, for despite my fantasy episode with Connie's mother, I had never cheated on Connie. True, I had experienced normal day-dreams over random females—this actress, that stewardess, some wide-eyed college girl—yet never would I have been unfaithful toward my lover. And not because I couldn't have. Certain women I had come in contact with had been quite aggressive, even predatory, but my loyalty had re-mained with Connie; doubly so, during this trying time of her impotence. It occurred to me, of course, to hit on Emily again, whom I still saw with and without Connie in innocent, companion-able fashion, but I felt that to stoke up embers I had labored so successfully to dampen would only lead to everybody's misery.

This is not to say that Connie was faithful. No, the sad truth was, on at least several occasions, she had succumbed to alien wiles, bedding surrepti-tiously with actors and authors alike.

"What do you want me to say?" she wept one three A.M. when I had caught her in a tangle of contradicting alibis. "I only do it to assure myself I'm not some sort of a freak. That I still am able to have sex."

"You can have sex with anyone but me," I said, furious with feelings of injustice.

"Yes. You remind me of my brother."

"I don't want to hear that nonsense."

"I told you to sleep with other women."

"I've tried not to, but it looks as if I'm going to have to."

"Please. Do it. It's a curse," she sobbed.

It was truly a curse. For when two people love each other and are forced to separate because of an almost comical aberration, what else could it be? That I brought it on myself by developing a close relationship with her mother was undeniable. Perhaps it was my comeuppance for thinking I could entice and bed Emily Chasen, having already made whoopee with her offspring.

The sin of hubris, maybe. Me, Harold Cohen, guilty of hubris. A man who has never thought of himself in an order higher than rodent, nailed for hubris? Too hard to swallow. And yet we did separate. Painfully, we remained friends and went our individual ways. True, only ten city blocks lay between our residences and we spoke every other day, but the relationship was over. It was then, and only then, that I began to realize how much I had really adored Connie. Inevitably bouts of melancholy and anxiety accentuated my

Proustian haze of pain. I recalled all our fine moments together, our exceptional love-making, and in the solitude of my large apartment, I wept. I attempted to go out on dates, but again, inevitably, everything seemed flat. All the little groupies and secretaries that paraded through the bedroom left me empty; even worse than an evening alone with a good book. The world seemed truly stale and unprofitable; quite a dreary, awful place, until one day I got the stunning news that Connie's mother had left her husband and they were getting a divorce. Imagine that, I thought, as my heart beat faster than normal speed for the first time in ages. My parents fight like the Montagues and Capulets and stay together their whole lives. Connie's folks sip martinis and hug with true civility and, bingo, they're divorcing.

My course of action was now obvious. Trader Vic's. Now there could be no crippling obstacles in our path. Though it would be somewhat awkward as I had been Connie's lover, it held none of the overwhelming difficulties of the past. We were now two free agents. My dormant feelings for Emily Chasen, always smoldering, ignited once again. Perhaps a cruel twist of fate ruined my relationship with Connie, but nothing would stand in the way of my conquering her mother.

Riding the crest of the large economy-size hubris, I phoned Emily and made a date. Three days later we sat huddled in the dark of my favorite Polynesian restaurant, and loose from three Bahia's, she poured out her heart about the demise

200

of her marriage. When she got to the part about looking for a new life with less restraint and more creative possibilities, I kissed her. Yes, she was taken aback but she did not scream. She acted surprised, but I confessed my feelings toward her and kissed her again. She seemed confused but did not bolt from the table, outraged. By the third kiss I knew she would succumb. She shared my feelings. I took her to my apartment and we made love. The following morning, when the effects of the rum had worn off, she still looked magnificent to me and we made love again.

"I want you to marry me," I said, my eyes glazed over with adoration.

"Not really," she said.

"Yes," I said. "I'll settle for nothing less." We kissed and had breakfast, laughing and making plans. That day I broke the news to Connie, braced for a blow that never came. I had anticipated any number of reactions ranging from derisive laughter to outright fury, but the truth was Connie took it in charming stride. She herself was leading an active social life, going out with several attractive men, and had experienced great concern over her mother's future when the woman had gotten divorced. Suddenly a young knight had emerged to care for the lovely lady. A knight who still had a fine, friendly relationship with Connie. It was a stroke of good fortune all around. Connie's guilt over putting me through hell would be removed. Emily would be happy. I would be happy. Yes, Connie took it all in casual, good-humored stride, natural to her upbringing.

My parents, on the other hand, proceeded directly to the window of their tenth-story apartment and competed for leaping space.

"I never heard of such a thing," my mother wailed, rending her robe and gnashing her teeth.

"He's crazy. You idiot. You're crazy," my father said, looking pale and stricken.

"A fifty-five-year-old *shiksa!?*" my Aunt Rose shrieked, lifting the letter opener and bringing it to her eyes.

"I love her," I protested.

"She's more than twice your age," Uncle Louie yelled.

"So?"

"So it's not done," my father yelled, invoking the Torah.

"His girl friend's mother he's marrying?" Aunt Tillie yelped as she slid to the floor unconscious.

"Fifty-five and a *shiksa*," my mother screamed, searching now for a cyanide capsule she had reserved for just such occasions.

"What are they, Moonies?" Uncle Louie asked. "Do they have him hypnotized!?"

"Idiot! Imbecile," Dad screamed. Aunt Tillie regained consciousness, focused on me, remembered where she was, and passed out again. In the far corner, Aunt Rose was down on her knees intoning Sh'ma Yisroel.

"God will punish you, Harold," my father yelled. "God will cleave your tongue to the roof of your mouth and all your cattle and kine shall die and a tenth of all thy crops shall wither and . . ."

But I married Emily and there were no suicides. Emily's three children attended and a dozen or so friends. It was held in Connie's apartment and champagne flowed. My folks could not make it, a previous commitment to sacrifice a lamb taking precedence. We all danced and joked and the evening went well. At one point, I found myself in the bedroom with Connie alone. We kidded and reminisced about our relationship, its ups and downs, and how sexually attracted I had been to her.

"It was flattering," she said warmly.

"Well, I couldn't swing it with the daughter, so I carried off the mother." The next thing I knew, Connie's tongue was in my mouth. "What the hell are you doing?" I said, pulling back. "Are you drunk?"

"You turn me on like you can't believe," she said, dragging me down on the bed.

"What's gotten into you? Are you a nymphomaniac?" I said, rising, yet undeniably excited by her sudden aggressiveness.

"I have to sleep with you. If not now, then soon," she said.

"Me? Harold Cohen? The guy who lived with you? And loved you? Who couldn't get near you with a ten-foot pole because I became a version of Danny? Me you're hot for? Your brother symbol?"

"It's a whole new ball game," she said, pressing

close to me. "Marrying Mom has made you my father." She kissed me again and just before returning to the festivities said, "Don't worry, Dad, there'll be plenty of opportunities."

I sat on the bed and stared out the window into infinite space. I thought of my parents and wondered if I should abandon the theatre and return to rabbinical school. Through the half-open door I saw Connie and also Emily, both laughing and chatting with guests, and all I could mutter to myself as I remained a limp, hunched figure was an age-old line of my grandfather's which goes "Oy vey."

Confessions
of a Burglar

*(Following are excerpts from the soon to be pub-
lished memoirs of Virgil Ives, who is currently
serving the first of four consecutive ninety-nine-
year sentences for various felonies. Mr. Ives plans
on working with children when he gets out.)*

SURE I STOLE. Why not? Where I grew up, you
had to steal to eat. Then you had to steal to tip.
Lots of guys stole fifteen per cent, but I always
stole twenty, which made me a big favorite among
the waiters. On the way home from a heist, I'd
steal some pajamas to sleep in. Or if it was a hot
night, I'd steal underwear. It was a way of life.
I had a bad upbringing, you might say. My dad
was always on the run from the cops and I never
saw him out of disguise till I was twenty-two. For
years, I thought he was a short, bearded man with
dark glasses and a limp; actually, he was tall and
blond and resembled Lindbergh. He was a pro-

fessional bank robber, but sixty-five was the mandatory retirement age, so he had to get out. Spent his last few years in mail fraud, but the postal rates went up and he lost everything.

Mom was wanted, too. Of course in those days it wasn't the way it is now, with women demanding equal rights, and all. Back then, if a woman turned to crime the only opportunities open to her were blackmail and, once in a while, arson. Women were used in Chicago to drive getaway cars, but only during the drivers' strike, in 1926. Terrible strike. It lasted eight weeks, and whenever a gang pulled a job and ran out with the money they were forced to walk or take a cab.

I had a sister and two brothers. Jenny married money. Not an actual human being—it was a pile of singles. My brother Vic got in with a gang of plagiarists. He was in the middle of signing his name to "The Waste Land" when the feds surrounded the house. He got ten years. Some rich kid from a highfalutin family who signed Pound's "Cantos" got off on probation. That's the law for you. Charlie—that's my youngest brother—he's been a numbers runner, a fence, and a loan shark. Never could find himself. Eventually he was arrested for loitering. He loitered for seven years, till he realized it was not the kind of crime that brought in any money.

The first thing I ever stole was a loaf of bread. I was working for Rifkin's Bakery, where my job was to remove the jelly from doughnuts that had gone stale and transfer it to fresh goods. It was very exacting work, done with a rubber tube and a scalpel. If your hands shook, the jelly went on the floor and old man Rifkin would pull your hair. Arnold Rothstein, who we all looked up to, came in one day and said he wanted to get his hands on a loaf of bread but he absolutely refused to pay for it. He hinted that this was a chance for some smart kid to get into the rackets. I took that as a cue, and each day when I left I put one slice of rye under my coat, until after three weeks I had accumulated a whole loaf. On the way to Rothstein's office, I began to feel remorse, because even though I hated Rifkin his wife had once let me take home two seeds from a roll when my uncle was dying. I tried to return the bread, but I got caught while I was trying to figure out which loaf each slice belonged to. The next thing I knew, I was in Elmira Reformatory.

Elmira was a tough joint. I escaped five times. Once I tried to sneak out in the back of a laundry truck. The guards got suspicious, and one of them poked me with his stick and asked me what the hell I was doing lying around in a hamper. I looked him right in the eye and said, "I'm some shirts." I could tell he was dubious. He kept pacing back and forth and staring at me. I guess I got a little panicky. "I'm some *shirts*," I told him. "Some denim work shirts—blue ones." Before I could say another word, my arms and legs were manacled and I was back in stir.

I learned everything I knew about crime at Elmira: how to pick pockets, how to crack a safe, how to cut glass—all the fine points of the trade. For instance, I learned (and not even all professional criminals know this) that in the event of a shootout with the cops, the cops are always allowed the first two shots. It's just the way it's done. Then you return fire. And if a cop says, "We have the house surrounded, come out with your hands up," you don't just shoot wildly. You say, "I'd prefer not to," or "I'd rather not at this particular time." There's a right way to do these things, but today . . . Well, why go into all that?

For the next few years of my life I was the best damn burglar you ever saw. People talk about Raffles, but Raffles had his style and I had mine. I had lunch with Raffles' son once. Nice guy. We ate at the old Lindy's. He stole the pepper mill. I stole the silverware and napkins. Then he took the ketchup bottle. I took his hat. He got my umbrella and tiepin. When we left we kidnapped a waiter. It was quite a haul. The original Raffles began as a cat burglar. (I couldn't do that, because the whiskers make me sneeze.) He'd dress up in this beat-up cat suit and dart over rooftops. In the end, he was caught by two guys from Scotland Yard dressed as dogs. I suppose you've heard of the Kissing Bandit? He'd break into a joint and rob the victim, and if it was a woman he'd kiss her. It was sad the way the law finally nailed him. He had two old dowagers tied up and he was prancing in front of them singing "Gimme a Little Kiss, Will Ya, Huh?" when he slipped on a footstool and fractured his pelvis.

Those boys made all the headlines, but I pulled off some capers that the police never did figure out. Once, I entered a mansion, blew the safe, and removed six thousand dollars while a couple slept in the same room. The husband woke up when the dynamite went off, but when I assured him that the entire proceeds would go to the Boys' Clubs of America he went back to sleep. Cleverly, I left behind some fingerprints of Franklin D. Roosevelt, who was President then. Another time, at a big diplomatic cocktail party, I stole a woman's diamond necklace while we were shaking hands. Used a vacuum cleaner on her—an old Hoover. Got her necklace and earrings. Later, when I opened the bag I found some false teeth there, which belonged to the Dutch Ambassador.

My most beautiful job, though, was when I bróke into the British Museum. I knew that the entire floor of the Rare Gems Room was wired and the slightest pressure on it would set off an alarm. I was lowered in upside down by a rope from the skylight, so I wouldn't touch the ground. I came through neat as you please, and in a minute I was hovering over the famous Kittridge Diamonds in their display case. As I pulled out my glass cutter a little sparrow flew in through the skylight and landed on the floor. The alarm sounded and eight squad cars arrived. I got ten years. The sparrow got twenty to life. The bird was out in six months, on probation. A year later, he was picked up in Fort Worth for pecking Rabbi Morris Klugfein into a state of semiconsciousness.

What advice would I give the average homeowner to protect himself against burglars? Well, the first thing is to keep a light on in the house when you go out. It must be at least a sixty-watt bulb; anything less and the burglar will ransack the house, out of contempt for the wattage. Another good idea is to keep a dog, but this is not foolproof. Whenever I was about to rob a house with a dog in it, I threw in some dog food mixed with Seconal. If that didn't work, I'd grind up equal parts of chopped meat and a novel by Theodore Dreiser. If it happens that you are going out of town and must leave your house unguarded, it's a good idea to put a cardboard silhouette of yourself in the window. Any silhouette will do. A Bronx man once placed a cardboard silhouette of Montgomery Clift in his window and then went to Kutsher's for the weekend. Later, Montgomery Clift himself happened to walk by and saw the silhouette, which caused him great anxiety. He attempted to strike up a conversation, and when it failed to answer for seven hours Clift returned to California and told his friends that New Yorkers were snobbish.

If you surprise an intruder in the act of bur-glarizing your home, do not panic. Remember, he is as frightened as you are. One good device is to rob *him*. Seize the initiative and relieve the burglar of his watch and wallet. Then he can get into your bed while you make a getaway. Trapped by this defense, I once wound up living in Des Moines for six years with another man's wife and three children, and only left when I was fortunate enough to surprise another burglar, who took my place. The six years I lived with that family were very happy ones, and I often look back on them with affection, although there is also much to be said for working on a chain gang.

About the Author

After he was ejected from both New York University and City College, WOODY ALLEN turned to a professional writing career, at first for television and comedians. In 1964 he decided to become a comedian himself.

In addition to his numerous nightclub and television appearances, Mr. Allen has made three comedy record albums of live concert appearances and somehow found the time to write two long-running hits for Broadway, *Don't Drink the Water* and *Play It Again Sam* (the latter starring himself in both the play and the later film version). His first film script, written in 1964, was the enormously popular *What's New Pussycat?* He has also written, directed and starred in seven films to date: *Take the Money and Run, Bananas, Everything You Always Wanted to Know about Sex, Sleeper, Love and Death, Annie Hall* and *Manhattan*.

Mr. Allen has written and appeared in his own television specials and is a frequent contributor to *The New Yorker,* among other periodicals.

His one regret in life is that he is not someone else.

On the Lighter Side...

Allow at least 4 weeks for delivery.   TA-49

The
Best Modern Fiction
from
BALLANTINE